Exclusive Onl

As our valued reader, your purchase of this book includes access to exclusive online resources designed to enhance your learning experience. These resources can be downloaded from our website, www.vibrantpublishers.com, and are created to help you apply Inclusive Leadership concepts effectively.

Online resources for this book include the following essential tools and templates:

- Implementation template for inclusive leadership
- Inclusive leadership auditing tool
- Inclusive leadership industry insights
- Organizational assessment guide
- Survey questions
- Video resources for inclusive leadership

Why these online resources are valuable:

- **Practical application:** The ready-to-use tools and templates simplify complex processes.
- **Step-by-step guidance:** They enable a clear understanding of concepts, efficient implementation of techniques, and skill refinement.
- **Enhanced learning experience:** They reinforce knowledge with structured guides and additional resources.

How to access your online resources:

1. **Visit the website:** Go to www.vibrantpublishers.com
2. **Find your book:** Navigate to the book's product page via the "Shop" menu or by searching for the book title in the search bar.
3. **Request the resources:** Scroll down to the "Request Sample Book/Online Resource" section.
4. **Enter your details:** Enter your preferred email ID and select "Online Resource" as the resource type. Lastly, select "user type" and submit the request.
5. **Check your inbox:** The resources will be delivered directly to your email.

Alternatively, for quick access: simply scan the QR code below to go directly to the product page and request the online resources by filling in the required details.

bit.ly/il-slm

Happy learning!

SELF-LEARNING MANAGEMENT SERIES

INCLUSIVE LEADERSHIP ESSENTIALS
YOU ALWAYS WANTED TO KNOW

A guide that prepares you to lead
with empathy and strategic insight

DR. DEANNA KIMBREL-HOPKINS

INCLUSIVE LEADERSHIP ESSENTIALS YOU ALWAYS WANTED TO KNOW

First Edition

Copyright © 2025, by Vibrant Publishers LLC, USA. All rights reserved. No part of this publication may be reproduced or distributed in any form or by any means, or stored in a database or retrieval system, without the prior permission of the publisher.

Published by Vibrant Publishers LLC, USA, www.vibrantpublishers.com

Paperback ISBN 13: 978-1-63651-476-5
Ebook ISBN 13: 978-1-63651-477-2
Hardback ISBN 13: 978-1-63651-478-9

Library of Congress Control Number: 2025935452

This publication is designed to provide accurate and authoritative information regarding the subject matter covered. The Author has made every effort in the preparation of this book to ensure the accuracy of the information. However, information in this book is sold without warranty, either expressed or implied. The Author or the Publisher will not be liable for any damages caused or alleged to be caused either directly or indirectly by this book.

All trademarks and registered trademarks mentioned in this publication are the property of their respective owners. These trademarks are used for editorial and educational purposes only, without intent to infringe upon any trademark rights. This publication is independent and has not been authorized, endorsed, or approved by any trademark owner.

Vibrant Publishers' books are available at special quantity discounts for sales promotions, or for use in corporate training programs. For more information, please write to bulkorders@vibrantpublishers.com

Please email feedback/corrections (technical, grammatical, or spelling) to spellerrors@vibrantpublishers.com

Vibrant publishes in a variety of print and electronic formats and by print-on-demand. Some material included with standard print versions of this book may not be included in e-books or in print-on-demand. To access the complete catalog of Vibrant Publishers, visit www.vibrantpublishers.com

SELF-LEARNING MANAGEMENT SERIES

TITLE	PAPERBACK* ISBN
BUSINESS AND ENTREPRENEURSHIP	
BUSINESS COMMUNICATION ESSENTIALS	9781636511634
BUSINESS ETHICS ESSENTIALS	9781636513324
BUSINESS LAW ESSENTIALS	9781636511702
BUSINESS PLAN ESSENTIALS	9781636511214
BUSINESS STRATEGY ESSENTIALS	9781949395778
ENTREPRENEURSHIP ESSENTIALS	9781636511603
INTERNATIONAL BUSINESS ESSENTIALS	9781636513294
PRINCIPLES OF MANAGEMENT ESSENTIALS	9781636511542
COMPUTER SCIENCE AND TECHNOLOGY	
BLOCKCHAIN ESSENTIALS	9781636513003
MACHINE LEARNING ESSENTIALS	9781636513775
PYTHON ESSENTIALS	9781636512938
DATA SCIENCE FOR BUSINESS	
BUSINESS INTELLIGENCE ESSENTIALS	9781636513362
DATA ANALYTICS ESSENTIALS	9781636511184
FINANCIAL LITERACY AND ECONOMICS	
COST ACCOUNTING & MANAGEMENT ESSENTIALS	9781636511030
FINANCIAL ACCOUNTING ESSENTIALS	9781636510972
FINANCIAL MANAGEMENT ESSENTIALS	9781636511009
MACROECONOMICS ESSENTIALS	9781636511818
MICROECONOMICS ESSENTIALS	9781636511153
PERSONAL FINANCE ESSENTIALS	9781636511849
PRINCIPLES OF ECONOMICS ESSENTIALS	9781636512334

*Also available in Hardback & Ebook formats

SELF-LEARNING MANAGEMENT SERIES

TITLE	PAPERBACK* ISBN

HR, DIVERSITY, AND ORGANIZATIONAL SUCCESS

DIVERSITY, EQUITY, AND INCLUSION ESSENTIALS	9781636512976
DIVERSITY IN THE WORKPLACE ESSENTIALS	9781636511122
HR ANALYTICS ESSENTIALS	9781636510347
HUMAN RESOURCE MANAGEMENT ESSENTIALS	9781949395839
ORGANIZATIONAL BEHAVIOR ESSENTIALS	9781636512303
ORGANIZATIONAL DEVELOPMENT ESSENTIALS	9781636511481

LEADERSHIP AND PERSONAL DEVELOPMENT

DECISION MAKING ESSENTIALS	9781636510026
INDIA'S ROAD TO TRANSFORMATION: WHY LEADERSHIP MATTERS	9781636512273
LEADERSHIP ESSENTIALS	9781636510316
TIME MANAGEMENT ESSENTIALS	9781636511665

MODERN MARKETING AND SALES

CONSUMER BEHAVIOR ESSENTIALS	9781636513263
DIGITAL MARKETING ESSENTIALS	9781949395747
MARKETING MANAGEMENT ESSENTIALS	9781636511788
MARKET RESEARCH ESSENTIALS	9781636513744
SALES MANAGEMENT ESSENTIALS	9781636510743
SERVICES MARKETING ESSENTIALS	9781636511733
SOCIAL MEDIA MARKETING ESSENTIALS	9781636512181

*Also available in Hardback & Ebook formats

SELF-LEARNING MANAGEMENT SERIES

TITLE	PAPERBACK* ISBN
OPERATIONS MANAGEMENT	
AGILE ESSENTIALS	9781636510057
OPERATIONS & SUPPLY CHAIN MANAGEMENT ESSENTIALS	9781949395242
PROJECT MANAGEMENT ESSENTIALS	9781636510712
STAKEHOLDER ENGAGEMENT ESSENTIALS	9781636511511
CURRENT AFFAIRS	
DIGITAL SHOCK	9781636513805

*Also available in Hardback & Ebook formats

About the Author

Dr. DeAnna Kimbrel-Hopkins has established herself as a strategic and transformational leader, accumulating over 17 years of experience across various sectors, including Higher Education, Corporate, and Government. Her initiatives have focused on driving change in leadership, organizational culture, diversity, equity, and inclusion. Dr. Kimbrel-Hopkins is recognized as a visionary leader whose passion for diversity, equity, and inclusion was reignited by the social unrest of 2020, prompting her to spearhead strategic initiatives aimed at fostering sustainable, systemic change within organizations.

A graduate of the Rochester City School District, Dr. Kimbrel-Hopkins holds a bachelor's degree in communication and international business from the State University at Buffalo, a master's degree in communication and marketing from the Rochester Institute of Technology, and a Doctoral degree in Management and Organizational Leadership from the University of Phoenix.

In recent role as Chief Diversity Officer and Director of the Office of DEI for Monroe County in New York State, Dr. Kimbrel-Hopkins led diversity, equity, and inclusion efforts. She has also played pivotal roles in shaping DEI and leadership strategies at notable organizations such as Paychex, Sears, and the Rochester Institute of Technology. Beyond her corporate roles, she guides a team of consultants at Kimbrel Management Consulting, assisting small to mid-sized organizations in developing robust structures and strategies concerning leadership, organizational culture, and diversity, equity, and inclusion.

Known for her charismatic personality and dynamic capabilities, Dr. DeAnna Kimbrel-Hopkins excels in fostering inclusive environments wherever her work takes her. She currently resides in Rochester, NY, with her husband and family.

What Experts Say About This Book!

Inclusive Leadership Essentials does a fantastic job of providing the foundational knowledge for students to prepare themselves to be inclusive leaders in their future careers. Beyond providing a great foundation of understanding, the book is applied, practical, and connected to the real day-to-day challenges and opportunities that employees face.

– **Kristie Moergen, Ph.D., Assistant Professor,
Iowa State University**

Kimbrel-Hopkins makes the case for why workforce diversity strengthens organizations and how leaders can best ensure that people feel valued and appreciated for who they are and what they contribute. It is written clearly and in an easy-to-understand fashion, with illustrative examples and potent applications. It is an excellent primer for getting started and also a valuable resource for experienced practitioners and leaders who wish to address both systemic and personal biases.

– **Barry Z. Posner, Chair of Management and Entrepreneurship Department at Santa Clara University**

Dr. DeAnna Kimbrel-Hopkins offers a valuable and practical guide for inclusive leadership, rooted in lived experience and strategic insight. Inclusive Leadership Essentials is a great starting point for professionals and organisations committed to advancing equity, building trust, and leading with purpose.

– **Jiten Patel, Director and Head of Operations
at Diversity Marketplace**

Table of Contents

1   DEI and Leadership   1

    1.1 A Review of Diversity, Equity, and Inclusion 2
    1.2 A Review of Affirmative Action 6
    1.3 A Review of Workplace Discrimination and Bias 9
    1.4 Biases in the Workplace 12
    1.5 Benefits of an Inclusive Workforce 16
    Chapter Summary 18
    Quiz 19

2   Introducing Inclusive Leadership   23

    2.1 Defining Inclusive Leadership 24
    2.2 Applying Leadership Styles 27
    2.3 Cultural Intelligence and Leadership 30
    Chapter Summary 34
    Quiz 35
    Case Study 38

3   Power and Justice in Inclusive Leadership   41

    3.1 Power, Justice, and Influence 41
    3.2 Leadership and Equity 49
    3.3 Workplace Culture and Leadership 52
    Chapter Summary 59
    Quiz 61

4 Inclusion as a Leadership Strategy   65

4.1 Strategic Inclusion: Communication Across Cultural Differences 66
4.2 Communication and Cultural Inclusion 68
4.3 Systemically Leveraging Cultural Differences 75
Chapter Summary 79
Quiz 80
Case Study 83

5 Organizations' Role in Developing Leaders   89

5.1 Leadership: Inherited or Developed? 90
5.2 Purpose Driven Leadership 96
Chapter Summary 99
Quiz 100

6 Implementing Different Leadership Traits   103

6.1 Authentic and Empathetic Leadership 104
6.2 Self-Leadership, Awareness, and Bias 109
6.3 Cultivating a Unique Inclusive Leadership Identity 112
6.4 Consequences of Exclusionary Leadership 113
Chapter Summary 115
Quiz 116

7 Building Effective Teams as an Inclusive Leader   121

7.1 Elements of an Effective Team 122
7.2 Sourcing and Selecting the Right Team Members 124
7.3 Establishing Team Norms 129
7.4 Communicating Effectively Across Diverse Teams 131
Chapter Summary 135
Quiz 136

8 Using Influence and Measuring Performance — 139

8.1 Assessing Performance 140
8.2 Using Influence as a Tool to Increase Performance 141
8.3 Goal Setting: A Powerful Tool for Influence 141
8.4 Retaining Diverse Populations 143
8.5 Professional Development: A Tool to Increase Equity 145
Chapter Summary 149
Quiz 150

9 Developing and Implementing a Sustainable DEI Leadership Plan — 153

9.1 Developing and Implementing a DEI Framework 154
9.2 Gaining Buy-in from Senior Leadership 157
9.3 Vetting and Communicating Your DEI Framework 159
9.4 Measuring Outcomes 162
Chapter Summary 164
Quiz 165

Book Recap — 169

Glossary — 177

Bibliography — 181

Further reading — 187

Introduction to the Book

Unlocking the full potential of inclusive leadership has become more crucial than ever for achieving organizational success and sustainability. As businesses become more diverse and increasingly embrace the importance of diversity and inclusion, leaders are progressively tasked with the pivotal responsibility of creating equitable and inclusive work environments that foster growth and unity. This book is meticulously designed to guide HR professionals, business leaders, and organizational managers by equipping them with the essential tools and insights needed to effectively implement best practices that not only promote but also enhance inclusion within their organizations. By providing leaders with these strategic tools, organizations can cultivate a culture of respect, innovation, and productivity, ultimately empowering team members to become more resilient, adaptable, and forward-thinking.

The journey begins with this book offering a comprehensive fundamental education on understanding the intricate roots of DEI (Diversity, Equity, and Inclusion) and leadership within the workplace context. By grasping the true significance and transformative power of inclusive leadership, leaders bear the responsibility of gaining acceptance and appreciation for diverse backgrounds, unique perspectives, and varying experiences that team members bring to the table. Creating a workplace culture where differences are not only respected but also actively celebrated is essential for fostering a thriving and dynamic organization. Leveraging the comprehensive insights and practical guidance provided within this book, leaders will have the invaluable tools to cultivate an environment that is intentionally equitable, consistently innovative, and genuinely inclusive.

Furthermore, this book provides guidance on how to develop and sustain effective communication, promote seamless collaboration, and embrace the creation of spaces where everyone feels a profound sense of belonging and purpose. Included are strategies meticulously designed to increase access to a wide array of opportunities and development, ensuring equitable advancement for all. Additionally, implementing fair policies and practices guarantees that every employee feels valued, respected, and empowered. This comprehensive approach not only enhances team morale by fostering a sense of community and ownership but also drives organizational success by harnessing the full spectrum of diverse talents and ideas available. This book educates leaders to not only embrace DEI but to recognize it as a dynamic business initiative that goes above and beyond mere box-ticking. It positions DEI as a vital component in building organizations that are not just resilient but also agile, robust, and capable of thriving amidst the complexities of modern society and work environments.

Who Can Benefit From This Book?

- HR professionals, business leaders, and organizational managers can significantly benefit from the teaching of this book. This is a tool that is well developed to give leaders the insights to effectively implement strategies that not only promote but also strategically embed inclusion within their organizations. With these strategic tools, they can foster a culture of respect, innovation, and productivity, empowering team members to become more resilient, adaptable, and equity-first thinking.
- Additionally, team members at all organizational levels can gain a deeper understanding of DEI principles, as the book provides guidance on developing effective communication, promoting collaboration, and creating spaces where everyone feels a unique sense of belonging and purpose. By embracing these inclusive leadership practices, organizations can hone in on diverse talents and ideas, positioning themselves for success in the evolving business landscape.

How to Use This Book?

The book acts as a comprehensive tool, meticulously developed to equip leaders with essential insights needed to effectively implement strategies that not only promote inclusion but also strategically embed it within their organizations' core operations and culture.

- HR professionals, business leaders, and organizational managers can utilize this book to implement strategic inclusion and leadership strategies.
- As an emerging business leader, Chapter One provides a review of the foundations of DEI in the US.
- For the leader creating a strategic leadership approach, Chapter Two reviews different leadership styles and how to increase cultural awareness.
- For the leader looking to balance power, privilege, and communication, Chapters Three and Four provide knowledge on how to navigate power, justice, influence, and cultural communication.
- Through effective communication awareness, Chapter Five provides context that empowers team members to enhance their ability to become more resilient and adaptable while fostering an equity-first mentality in their everyday professional activities.
- Using teachings of empathy, Chapter Six explores how, by embracing inclusive leadership practices and incorporating them into the organizational fabric, organizations are investing in their team's personal and professional growth.

- If you are charged with building effective teams, Chapter Seven explores finding the best team members and establishing team norms.
- For the more established leader who struggles with data and results, Chapters Eight & Nine provide tactics to use data to track performance, make decisions, and use strategic frameworks to gain organizational buy-in.

Chapter 1
DEI and Leadership

Key Learning Objectives
- Building a culture of DEI
- Prioritizing DEI in the workplace
- Affirmative action in a DEI era
- Discrimination in the workplace
- Psychological safety in the workplace
- The benefits of an inclusive workplace

Chapter one serves as an introduction to Diversity, Equity, and Inclusion (DEI) and Leadership, defining them as frameworks aimed at enhancing organizational processes and functions. This chapter delineates essential terms, theories, and methodologies essential for the integration of these concepts. Its objective is to enrich the reader's comprehension of the definitions, developmental trajectory, divergent perspectives, fundamental functions, and obstacles linked to comprehending and executing crucial strategies related to DEI and leadership.

1.1 A Review of Diversity, Equity, and Inclusion

1.1.1 An evolving US population

The demographic makeup of the United States is rapidly changing. According to Figure 1.1, for the first time in 1990, the number of individuals identifying solely as White started to decrease. Those identifying exclusively as non-Hispanic, White without any other racial identification, decreased by more than 30% from 1990 to 2020.

Figure 1.1 The shrinking white population in the US

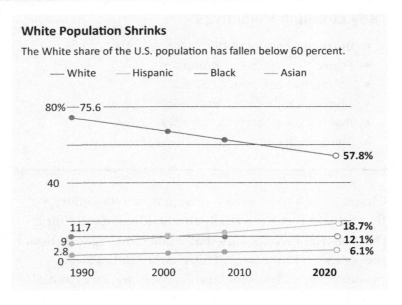

Source: Bureau, US Census. "Census.Gov | U.S. Census Bureau Homepage." Census.Gov, https://www.census.gov/en.html.

According to data from the latest census, the U.S. demographics have shifted towards a more diverse profile.[1]

---

1. Bureau, US Census. "Census.Gov." Census.gov. Accessed April 1, 2024. https://www.census.gov

With an estimated population of around 331 million people, this trend is becoming more pronounced. We can see that:

- Approximately 76.3% identify as White
- About 13.4% identify as Black or African American
- Roughly 5.9% identify as Asian
- Around 1.3% identify as American Indian or Alaska Native
- Merely 0.2% identify as Native Hawaiian or other Pacific Islander
- Furthermore, roughly 18.5% of the population identify as Hispanic or Latino of any race.

A major shift currently taking place in the United States is that it is becoming a majority-minority society. This can be seen in the decrease of the White population, which has dropped below 60% for the first time in American History, decreasing from 63.7 percent in 2010 to 57.8 percent in 2020. Also, the present American population under 18 years old comprises a majority of people of color, making up 52.7 percent.

- The demographic change in the population indicates a progressing, diverse, and inclusive society.
- This transformation underscores the significance of embracing multiculturalism and understanding diverse perspectives.
- The declining percentage of White individuals emphasizes the ongoing need to advance equality and diversity across society.
- As the population diversifies, it is crucial for policies and institutions to adjust to effectively cater to the needs of a multicultural population.

- Embracing this diversity can foster a more lively and dynamic society where different voices and experiences are appreciated and honored.

The American population is aging. The current median age in the US is around 38 years old.[2] This shift means that the generational makeup of the country is changing and largely consists of millennials and Gen Z who make up a significant portion of the overall population. Immigration also plays a significant factor in forming the current demographics.

As these demographic dynamics evolve, it's important for lawmakers and organizational leaders to adapt to meet the diverse needs of the new face of the US population. This need places a particular emphasis on intentional strategies related to DEI in the places where people work and live.

1.1.2 Building a culture of DEI

Building a culture of DEI is the responsibility of everyone. Contributing to a fair and just environment where everyone feels welcome is the key ingredient to sustainable DEI practices. However, if you are a leader, that responsibility becomes even more important and mandatory. This is done by taking the proper steps to build a culture of Diversity, Equity, and Inclusion (DEI). Below are some key points to consider when implementing DEI principles:

- Diversity includes all the differences that exist within a group of people. These differences can be seen or hidden, such as race, gender, age, sexual orientation,

---

[2]. Costanza, David P., Daniel M. Ravid, and Andrew J. Slaughter. "A Distributional Approach to Understanding Generational Differences: What Do You Mean They Vary?" *Journal of Vocational Behavior* 127 (June 2021): 103585. https://doi.org/10.1016/j.jvb.2021.103585.

religion, and abilities. Diversity provides different perspectives and experiences that positively impact a community or organization.

- Equity refers to the processes and policies put in place to ensure all team members have access to resources and opportunities to thrive in the workplace.
- Inclusion is intentionally cultivating a work environment where team members are welcomed, empowered, and feel a sense of belonging.

1.1.3 Prioritizing DEI in the workplace

DEI isn't a new concept or phenomenon in the US, but rather a recurring issue that has taken on many shapes and forms for several decades. The origins of DEI are rooted in the Civil Rights Movement of the 1960s, where activists advocated for equal rights for African Americans. This movement led to the implementation of "affirmative action laws." These laws sought to limit the impact of discrimination by increasing opportunities for marginalized groups, like women and people of color.

The Civil Rights Movement began in the 1950s and throughout the 1960s. This period of time was marked by protests, marches, and other forms of civil resilience. Leaders of this movement include Martin Luther King Jr., Rosa Parks, and Malcolm X, who fought for equal rights and opportunities for those most impacted by the status quo like women and African Americans. The Civil Rights Act of 1964 and the Voting Rights Act of 1965 are landmark legislations that are still relevant today.[3]

---

3. Costanza, David P., Daniel M. Ravid, and Andrew J. Slaughter. "A Distributional Approach to Understanding Generational Differences: What Do You Mean They Vary?" *Journal of Vocational Behavior* 127 (June 2021): 103585. https://doi.org/10.1016/j.jvb.2021.103585.

1.2 A Review of Affirmative Action

1.2.1 Affirmative action in a DEI era

Implemented in the 1960s, affirmative action is a policy that seeks to address historical and systemic discrimination by giving preferential treatment to individuals from underrepresented groups, such as women, people of color, and individuals with disabilities.[4] This can include outreach programs, quotas, and other initiatives designed to bring forth new opportunities for marginalized individuals. The policy has been a topic of debate for several decades in the United States. Today, according to Figure 1.2, although many Americans are aware of the term, affirmative action, they are unaware of its importance and function in the workplace. The Affirmative Action policy was developed by the federal government to protect the human rights of vulnerable populations of people in the United States.

Figure 1.2 Awareness and understanding of affirmative action

Source: Gramlich, John. "Americans and Affirmative Action: How the Public Sees the Consideration of Race in College Admissions, Hiring." Pew Research Center (blog), June 16, 2023. https://www.pewresearch.org/

---

4. Lippert-Rasmussen, Kasper. *Making Sense of Affirmative Action*. New York: Oxford University Press, 2020.

Despite this mix of opinions, affirmative action still plays an important role in American society. The policy has been challenged several times in the Supreme Court but is still upheld.[5] However, how it is implemented and its impact differs across organizations. Some organizations have put plans in place to move diversity efforts forward while others just use it as a check-the-box mechanism.

Many argue that affirmative action is unfair and offers reverse discrimination as some groups get certain privileges over others. On the other hand, others in support of the policy state that the privileges provided by the policy are considered equity. These privileges give people opportunities that they were historically deprived of, and are necessary to mitigate the impact of discrimination and racism. Affirmative action continues to be complex and controversial in the workplace. However, affirmative action is a policy used to help forward DEI and holds people accountable because of the weight of the law it carries.

Through the 1980s, words like "diversity" and "multiculturalism" became very popular in the workplace as many organizations started to see the benefits of a diverse workforce. With this, many organizations implemented various programs to help people gain more cultural competence. However, actual change around equity and opportunity was insignificant.

1.2.2 The social unrest of 2020

Many organizations developed and worked on DEI inconsistently and with little results until the emergence of the social unrest of 2020. During this time, many protests and social movements arose. This was also a time when people

---

5. Lippert-Rasmussen, Kasper. *Making Sense of Affirmative Action*. New York: Oxford University Press, 2020.

started to advocate for racial equity through a movement entitled "Black Lives Matter".

This movement was sparked by a police-related murder of an African American man, George Floyd. This incident caused activism across the country and the world. Many people protested and called for justice to address social inequities, police brutality, and mass criminalization of people of color.[6]

The COVID-19 pandemic also became a phenomenon that further exposed social and economic disparities for people of marginalized backgrounds in areas such as healthcare, education, and housing. This caused people to react by protesting for a real change in the historical conditions that impacted people from certain backgrounds for hundreds of years.[7] These social issues caused organizations to respond aggressively by implementing programs, leadership positions, and investments to address workplace discrimination, harassment, and equity.

1.2.3 Challenges to DEI in 2025

In 2025, Diversity, Equity, and Inclusion (DEI) initiatives came under increased scrutiny amid evolving political and cultural dynamics in the United States. Much of this attention stemmed from a national debate surrounding affirmative action, diversity-related policies, and differing interpretations of fairness. Some critics expressed concern that such initiatives might unintentionally disadvantage other groups, advocating instead for a merit-based approach. While this perspective emphasized equal treatment for all

---

[6]. Lackner, Mario, Uwe Sunde, and Rudolf Winter-Ebmer. "COVID-19 and the Forces behind Social Unrest." (2021).

[7]. Wood, Reed, Gina Yannitell Reinhardt, Babak RezaeeDaryakenari, and Leah C. Windsor. "Resisting lockdown: the influence of COVID-19 restrictions on social unrest." *International Studies Quarterly* 66, no. 2 (2022):

individuals, it was sometimes viewed as overlooking the broader context of historical and structural inequities.

Organizations committed to DEI work encountered a more complex operating environment, prompting many to reassess how they communicated their goals and measured progress. Greater emphasis was placed on demonstrating the practical outcomes of DEI efforts, including enhanced innovation, employee engagement, and improved market competitiveness. At the same time, community-based efforts continued to highlight individual experiences and share data-driven insights, aiming to foster understanding and address public concerns. These developments underscored the importance of clear communication, ongoing evaluation, and strategic adaptation in supporting inclusive practices during a time of increased scrutiny. As noted by Forbes, "Organizations that prioritize DEI not only advance equity but also uncover innovation and growth opportunities."[8]

1.3 A Review of Workplace Discrimination and Bias

1.3.1 Forms of workplace discrimination

Discrimination can manifest in many forms within the workplace. Some instances of discrimination can be more obvious than others. Common forms of discrimination can show up in the hiring, promotion, and selection processes at work. For example, when hiring decisions are based on factors unrelated to a person's qualifications, but rather on protected class categories like race, gender, age, religion, or sexual orientation, this is unlawful discrimination.

---

[8]. "Why DEI Matters More Than Ever in the Face of MEI," Forbes, October 11, 2024. https://www.forbes.com

When discrimination occurs repeatedly, it can create a hostile work environment. This looks like offensive comments or jokes, the use of derogatory language, or physical intimidation. Discrimination can also occur when a leader fails to provide reasonable accommodation for employees with disabilities or treats them unfairly because of their disability. Some examples of discrimination in the workplace are illustrated in Figure 1.3.

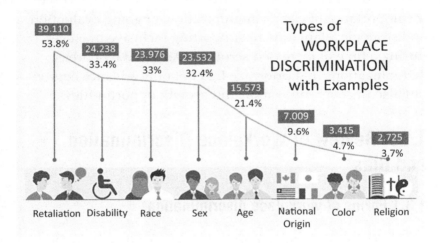

Figure 1.3 Types of workplace discrimination experiences with examples

Source: LiveAbout."Types of Discrimination in the Workplace." https://www.liveabout.com.

1.3.2 Discrimination Act of 1964

As an inclusive leader, it is important to be aware of the legislation put in place to protect people from discrimination and harassment. The Discrimination Act of 1964 was implemented to prevent and address insistences of individuals being treated unjustly because of physical differences. This law and others like it are also known as "anti-discrimination legislations", put in place to hold people accountable for unfair treatment.[9] These laws are intended to ensure people of diverse backgrounds have equal access to opportunity and the ability to thrive.

It is important for inclusive leaders to be aware of anti-discrimination laws as they create environments where equality and respect for all are valued. Groups of people who are legally protected from being harmed or harassed by laws, practices, and policies that discriminate against them due to a shared characteristic are called "protected classes."[10] Protected classes include:

- Race
- Gender identity, gender expression
- Religion (includes religious dress and grooming practices)
- Marital status
- Color
- Sex/gender (includes pregnancy, childbirth, breastfeeding, and/or related medical conditions)
- Sexual orientation

No organization is immune from the impact of discrimination. Therefore, it's important to know that discrimination can occur in any industry and at any job level, impacting individuals or groups. It is the responsibility of the organization to establish structures and strategies that ensure an anti-discriminatory work

---

9. Berg, Richard K. "Equal employment opportunity under the civil rights act of 1964." *Brook. L. Rev.* 31 (1964): 62.

10. Marin, Andy. "Inclusion as New Property Right: The Equality Act and Modernizing Anti-Discrimination Laws." *U. Pac. L. Rev.* 54 (2023): 507.

environment. Within the organization, the employee representative usually addresses these issues. However, more recently, you see DEI professionals within the organization handle these issues.

It is important as an inclusive leader to be aware of these policies and how they may impact your organization and work to ensure the voices of your team members are heard, they are being treated fairly, and there's action to eliminate discrimination or harassment in the workplace.

1.4 Biases in the Workplace

Implementing DEI practices can focus on many different aspects. However, a focus on bias can be an effective way to reduce workplace discrimination and harassment. Common forms of biases that can manifest in the workplace are:

1. **Unconscious bias:** This happens when someone may unconsciously like an applicant who is of the same religion.
2. **Affinity bias:** This happens when some people are favored because they share many of the same characteristics as others, which results in preferential treatment.
3. **Confirmation bias:** This happens when someone is only open to information that confirms their beliefs. For example, a person believes that a certain group of people is bad, and isn't open to learning information about that group of people that does not support their notion.
4. **The halo effect:** This happens when someone has a few positive traits, and it is assumed that the person has all positive traits. For example, if someone is

well-groomed, it may be presumed that they might be a good leader.

As an inclusive leader, it is important to address workplace biases as they can kill the culture of equity and inclusivity you are working toward. Mitigating workplace biases can be done in several ways. One common way organizations seek to address bias is through implementing diversity training programs that focus on unconscious bias and stereotypes, and bring awareness to DEI. Another tactic is the consistent review of policies and procedures to ensure they are unbiased and inclusive. It's important to ensure ongoing evaluations as that can help find trends that reveal gaps that perpetuate bias and correct accordingly.[11]

Presenting as an inclusive leader or role model who actively promotes diversity and inclusion can provide an example for peers and team members. When this behavior is demonstrated by senior leaders, a clear message is sent that bias is intolerable.

It's also important to ensure team members feel supported when confronting bias in the workplace. Resources should be provided to report instances of bias or discrimination. Establishing clear reporting procedures and holding confidentiality can encourage team members to disclose any instances of discrimination against them without fear of retaliation, ultimately creating a safer and more inclusive workplace for all.

Establishing a transparent hiring and promotion strategy based on merit and qualifications rather than personal biases is another way to address bias in the workplace. For example, performing blind recruitment processes that

---

11. Metinyurt, Tuğba, Michelle C. Haynes-Baratz, and Meg A. Bond. "A systematic review of interventions to address workplace bias: What we know, what we don't, and lessons learned." *New Ideas in Psychology* 63 (2021)

remove personal identifiers like name, gender, or race will help to mitigate biases and significantly impact hiring decisions. Also, activities such as implementing diverse interview panels and more job descriptions with inclusive language will attract a more diverse pool of applicants. Reducing bias at the recruitment stage can attract more diversity and reduce bias in how people are brought into organizations.[12]

Another effective way to decrease the impact of bias in the workplace is to develop a culture of communication and feedback. It's important that team members feel empowered to speak up and share their experiences. When people feel heard, they are more likely to be productive and build positive relationships.

1.4.1 Psychological safety in the workplace

Psychological safety is present in the workplace when coming to work threatens the well-being of team members. This is important as it plays an essential role in cultivating a culture based on DEI principles. Psychological safety leads to team members being more likely to disclose things about their identity, share ideas, and express issues without fear of retaliation or judgment.[13] When organizations are intentional about the psychological safety of their workforce, it can lead to increased innovation and decision-making.

You know your team feels psychologically safe when they are more comfortable asking questions, and giving feedback and suggestions, without fear of being judged or retaliation. Also, they are more likely to take risks, be creative, and

---

[12]. Hebl, Mikki, Shannon K. Cheng, and Linnea C. Ng. "Modern discrimination in organizations." *Annual Review of Organizational Psychology and Organizational Behavior* 7 (2020): 257-282.

[13]. Ge, Yuanqin. "Psychological safety, employee voice, and work engagement." *Social Behavior and Personality: an international journal* 48, no. 3 (2020): 1-7.

collaborate. This can lead to increased innovation and engagement. As an inclusive leader, you can create a psychologically safe work environment by communicating expectations clearly and supporting the well-being of team members.

As an inclusive leader, you play a crucial role in promoting psychological safety in work environments. Your leadership practices should go beyond being nice or avoiding conflict; they should focus on establishing a space where everyone on your team feels welcomed and included. You should promote a culture of questioning the status quo without fear or consequence. Team members should also feel safe, even when you can't put their suggestions into action.

As you continue on your journey to becoming an inclusive leader, there are several practices and principles required to be effective such as:

- Encourage open and honest communication with team members. Ensure regular meetings, formal or informal. Provide a safe space for people to address thoughts and/or negative experiences.[14]
- Take steps to build trust with team members. You should show your team members your trust in what they bring to the team by giving them autonomy. Establishing trust is fundamental to psychological safety and is furthered by consistency.[15]
- Promote collaboration among your team. This will allow you to create a sense of ownership. This will

---

14. Liu, Chang-E., Shengxian Yu, Yahui Chen, and Wei He. "Supervision incivility and employee psychological safety in the workplace." *International Journal of Environmental Research and Public Health* 17, no. 3 (2020): 840.

15. Kim, S., Lee, H., & Connerton, T. P. (2020). How psychological safety affects team performance: mediating role of efficacy and learning behavior. *Frontiers in psychology, 11*, 527909.

also lead to more cohesiveness and team members developing a sense of belonging.[16]
- Foster diversity and inclusion through recognizing and bringing awareness to the differences that exist in your team This starts with embracing diversity in perspectives, backgrounds, and experiences.[17]
- Provide the tools and resources that team members need to thrive. These may be opportunities for training, mentorship, or mental health navigation tools.[18] This will allow you to add equity to your leadership practices, and commitment to the well-being of your team members.
- It's important to realize that your journey as an inclusive leader is continuous and something that you must work toward on a consistent basis. There is no ending point, as people, society and cultures continue to evolve.

1.5 Benefits of an Inclusive Workforce

As discussed throughout this book, the many benefits of an inclusive work environment include increases in innovation, productivity, and profitability. However, there are additional benefits such as attracting and retaining top talent, and developing a more positive reputation in the marketplace. Intentionally implementing DEI practices seems like the best thing for all parties, but there are many

---

16. O'Donovan, Róisín, and Eilish McAuliffe. "A systematic review exploring the content and outcomes of interventions to improve psychological safety, speaking up and voice behaviour." *BMC health services research* 20 (2020): 1-11.

17. Sherf, E. N., Parke, M. R., & Isaakyan, S. (2021). Distinguishing voice and silence at work: Unique relationships with perceived impact, psychological safety, and burnout. *Academy of Management Journal, 64*(1), 114-148.

18. Edmondson, Amy C., and Derrick P. Bransby. "Psychological safety comes of age: Observed themes in an established literature." *Annual Review of Organizational Psychology and Organizational Behavior* 10 (2023): 55-78.

barriers to success such as a commitment from senior leaders, lack of dedicated resources, accountability, proper progress measures, organizational resistance and a lack of awareness.

Some steps in overcoming those barriers include:

1. Conduct an audit that will evaluate the current status of diversity, equity, and inclusion within your organization. Gather data on demographics, hiring practices, promotions, compensation, and employee feedback to establish a foundation for setting objectives and monitoring progress.[19]
2. Based on the DEI audit results, establish measurable and relevant goals. For instance, aim to increase underrepresented employees by 20% in the next two years or narrow the pay gap between different groups by 10% within a year.
3. Develop a committee or campaigns that are like-minded to spread your purpose and advocate for change throughout the organization.
4. Ensure that the senior leadership team supports your vision and the charter you put forth for change.

As an inclusive leader, it's imperative that you create space to grow more diverse and inclusive teams and talent pools, improve employee engagement, increase innovation, and enhance overall organizational effectiveness. You should be able to recognize that all employees need to have a sense of belonging and equitable access to opportunities for growth. This can be accomplished through creating policies and resources to support more inclusive work environments, and also being a role model for your organization.

---

[19]. Lubis, Muhlisah. "The Role of Communication and Employee Engagement in Promoting Inclusion in the Workplace: A Case Study in the Creative Industry." *Feedback International Journal of Communication* 1, no. 1 (2024): 1-15.

Chapter Summary

- To successfully implement DEI principles in business and society, it is important to embrace diversity.
- Equity will provide fair opportunities and treatment for all individuals, regardless of their background.
- Fostering inclusion is essential to a welcoming environment where everyone feels valued and respected.
- The affirmative action policies that emerged from the Civil Rights Movement combat discrimination and ensure more opportunities for underrepresented groups.
- The Black Lives Matter protests shed light on racism that still persists in society.
- Workplace discrimination is bias in hiring practices, promotion opportunities, harassment, and a lack of accommodations for individuals with disabilities.
- Recognizing and addressing biases is crucial in creating a more inclusive and equitable work environment.
- Establishing psychological safety within an organization is key to fostering open communication, trust, and innovation among team members.
- Embracing DEI also leads to increased innovation, higher productivity, and improved talent retention.
- Implementing sustainable DEI practices involves conducting regular audits, setting measurable goals, establishing committees, providing training, nurturing an inclusive culture, and securing support from senior leadership.

Quiz

1. Which of the following is indicated by the changing demographics in the US as being needed for DEI in communities and the workplace?
   a. Significance of embracing multiculturalism and understanding diverse perspectives.
   b. There is an ongoing need to advance equality and diversity across society.
   c. Policies and institutions must adjust to effectively cater to the needs of a multicultural population
   d. All of the above

2. Discrimination in the workplace only applies to those from protected classes, which doesn't include:
   a. Race
   b. Attire
   c. Religion (includes religious dress and grooming practices)
   d. Sex/gender (includes pregnancy, childbirth, breastfeeding, and/ or related medical conditions)

3. The Civil Rights Movement was a social and political movement in the United States that sought to end racial discrimination for:
   a. African Americans
   b. Women
   c. Children
   d. None of the above

4. Building a culture of Diversity, Equity, and Inclusion (DEI) within an organization or community is crucial for fostering a positive and thriving environment where all individuals feel respected and valued. This requires the organization to:
   a. Acknowledge and embrace the wide range of characteristics and backgrounds within the group, such as race, ethnicity, gender, age, sexual orientation, religion, and physical abilities.
   b. Ensure that everyone has equal access to opportunities, resources, and support, regardless of their background or identity.
   c. Create a welcoming and respectful environment where everyone feels valued and empowered to contribute their best work.
   d. All of the above

5. Discrimination is when an employer makes a hiring decision based on what factors?
   a. Attire
   b. Name
   c. Age
   d. All of the above

6. Ways to decrease workplace discrimination include:
   a. Open communication
   b. Fair treatment
   c. Resolving disputes
   d. All of the above

7. Bias still creeps into the workplace in many forms. The following are common forms of bias that can exist in the workplace except:
    a. Unconscious bias
    b. Affinity bias
    c. Confirmation bias
    d. Friendship bias

8. Ways to reduce bias in the workplace include:
    a. Implementing training programs
    b. Ignore behaviors
    c. Don't provide resources for everyone to be successful
    d. All the above

9. Promoting diversity and inclusion from leaders sets a positive example for the rest of the organization because:
    a. Leaders are the catalyst for change
    b. Diverse perspective at the top is important
    c. Representation matters
    d. All of the above

10. The Civil Rights movement was led by all the following prominent figures except:
   a. Martin Luther King Jr
   b. Rosa Parks
   c. Malcolm X
   d. Bob Marley

Answers

1 – d	2 – b	3 – a	4 – d	5 – d
6 – d	7 – d	8 – a	9 – d	10 – d

CHAPTER 2
Introducing Inclusive Leadership

Key Learning Objectives
- Defining inclusive leadership
- Understanding leadership styles
- Applying leadership styles
- Communicating your leadership style
- Cultural intelligence and leadership
- Equipping leaders with the right tools

Chapter two functions as an introduction to inclusive leadership, portraying it as a strategy to enhance leaders' effectiveness. This chapter covers crucial terms, theories, and methodologies necessary for incorporating these concepts. It aims to enhance the reader's understanding of the definitions, developmental path, varied viewpoints, core functions, and challenges associated with grasping and implementing important strategies linked to inclusive leadership.

2.1 Defining Inclusive Leadership

You hold a powerful place within your organization as an inclusive leader. Working across the organization to help team members embrace DEI will unlock the full potential of your team members and drive organizational success. Through your unique perspective and skill set, you can intentionally develop an environment where everyone feels valued. According to Figure 2.1, statistics show that potential employees are more attracted to employers based on leadership's comprehension of DEI.

Figure 2.1 How potential employees choose employers based on leadership qualities.

85% of business say that diversity drives the most innovative ideas

80% of workers indicated inclusion was important when choosing an employer

30% of companies with inclusion practices generated up to 30% higher revenue per person

Source: Bureau, US Census. "Census.Gov | U.S. Census Bureau Homepage." Census.Gov, https://www.census.gov/en.html.

As a leader, you should consistently promote open communication, empathy, and fairness. This will allow you to build relationships across the organization and increase trust and cohesiveness. This approach to leadership will not only boost employee morale and engagement but also inspire creativity. This can lead to better business results. Inclusive leadership is a mindset that can transform organizations and drive success while addressing the needs of a growing diverse workforce. The following will be effective in developing a growth mindset as an inclusive leader:

- **Encourage failure:** View failures and setbacks as opportunities for growth.
- **Embrace feedback:** Use feedback as a source of information for improvement. Constructive criticism will allow you to grow your leadership skills.
- **Build your resilience:** Build up the courage to persist in difficult situations.
- **Acknowledge growth:** Celebrate your growth and the growth of your team members as you hit milestones.
- **Commit to continuous learning:** Never stop learning and growing your leadership skills and be a role model for your team members.

2.1.1 Understanding leadership styles

As a leader, you must be aware of your leadership style. This awareness will allow you to develop your inclusive mindset more authentically.[20] Leadership styles are the different ways a leader can guide and inspire teams. Different approaches have diverse characteristics, strengths, and weaknesses that impact team dynamics and outcomes. Here are some key points to consider about common leadership styles:[21]

---

20. Zeng, Hao, Lijing Zhao, and Yixuan Zhao. "Inclusive leadership and taking-charge behavior: roles of psychological safety and thriving at work." *Frontiers in psychology* 11 (2020): 509644.

21. Supriadi, Oding, Zulkifli Musthan, R. Nurjehan Sa'odah, Yuyun Dwi Haryanti, M. Rafid Marwal, Agus Purwanto, Abdul Mufid et al. "Did transformational, transactional leadership style and organizational learning influence innovation capabilities of school teachers during covid-19 pandemic." *Systematic Reviews in Pharmacy* 11, no. 9 (2020): 299-311.

- **Autocratic leadership:**
  - The leader makes decisions independently without consulting the team.
  - Effective in emergencies or when quick decisions are necessary.
  - Can result in low morale and creativity among team members due to lack of involvement.
- **Democratic leadership:**
  - Leader involves the team in decision-making processes.
  - Fosters high engagement and motivation among team members.
  - Consensus building may take longer compared to autocratic leadership.
- **Transformational leadership:**
  - Leaders inspire and motivate the team toward a shared goal.
  - Encourages commitment and innovation among team members.
  - Requires a visionary leader to drive the team forward effectively.

2.1.2 Effective leadership competencies

It is crucial for leaders to be aware of the various leadership styles and their implications. Here are a few additional insights on effective competencies:[22]

---

[22]. Wuryani, Eni, A. Rodlib, Sri Sutarsib, N. Dewib, and Donny Arifb. "Analysis of decision support system on situational leadership styles on work motivation and employee performance." Management Science Letters 11, no. 2 (2021): 365-372.

- **Adaptability:** As a leader, you should be able to pivot when required to address the various challenges you will face as an inclusive leader
- **Situational leadership:** The most effective leadership style varies depending on the specific circumstances and the individuals involved.

2.2 Applying Leadership Styles

2.2.1 Mastering different leadership styles

As an inclusive leader, you must build your leadership tool kit. This will equip you with the resources to respond appropriately and effectively. For example, one approach is situational leadership. This style means that the leader can adapt depending on the situation and the people involved. This theory, developed by Paul Hersey and Kenneth Blanchard, suggests that effective leaders can adjust their leadership style to meet the needs of team members. When using this leadership style, you want to determine the needs of your team members. There are four main approaches that can be implemented through this lens: directing, coaching, supporting, and delegating.[23]

- **Directing:** Here, leaders provide team members with close and direct support. To be effective, leaders must implement clear communication strategies.
- **Coaching:** Here, leaders focus on cultivating the skills and abilities of team members. This is often done through feedback, support, and access to opportunities. This approach focuses on helping team members to reach their full capabilities.

---

23. Benmira, Sihame, and Moyosolu Agboola. "Evolution of leadership theory." *BMJ leader* (2021): leader-2020.

- **Delegating:** Working in collaboration is key to properly delegate among your team. This style allows you to empower and inspire your team to make key decisions.

2.2.2 Developing a leadership identity

Developing your leadership identity is essential on your inclusive leadership journey. As you continue to evolve you will discover new dimensions of your leadership identity. This will allow you to be more authentic and get closer to your purpose. Through self-reflection on your experiences and getting feedback from others, your leadership identity will become clearer and will allow you to be a more effective leader. According to Figure 2.2, honesty is the top leadership trait for effective leadership.

Figure 2.2 Traits of a good leader

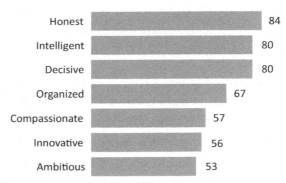

Source: *Pew Research Center." Pew Research Center, 11 Dec. 2024, https://www.pewresearch.org/.*

Once you've developed a strong leadership identity, it will be a road map when things are challenging times, helping you to stay the course and true to your values and purpose. On this journey of self-discovery and growth, you will be empowered to inspire and motivate those around you. Unlocking your authentic leadership identity will allow you to effectively lead through an inclusive lens[24].

As you continue to build upon your leadership journey, your identity becomes imperative. The following are principles that can be implemented in your daily routine to get closer to your goals:

- **Embrace self-awareness:** Become aware of your strengths and weaknesses and continue to develop them through authenticity and transparency. This will allow you to improve your decision-making and build better teams.
- **Set clear expectations:** Setting clear expectations will be effective in practicing fairness among your team and working toward more equity in your space.
- **Align values and leadership approach:** Building trust is key to your growth as an inclusive leader and requires that you ensure alignment of values with your team and organization.

2.2.3 Communicating your leadership style

Next, you need to be able to effectively communicate your leadership style. This will also allow you to build trust and credibility within your organization and among your team members. When you can clearly share your values, vision, and expectations, you are more likely to move forward your plan of action around DEI. It is also important that you

---

24. Owen, Julie E. "Deepening leadership identity development." *New directions for student leadership* 2023, no. 178 (2023): 11-20.

practice active listening.[25] According to Figure 2.3, effective communication is the top expectation employees have for leaders. However, only 42% of the surveyed participants stated that their company had effective communication methods.

Figure 2.3 Effective communication is #1 among employee expectations

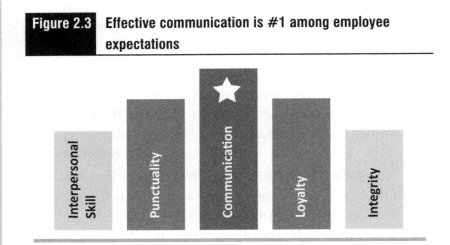

Source: *Employee Communication during the COVID-19 Pandemic.* https://www.alight.com/blog/employee-communication-coronavirus

2.3 Cultural Intelligence and Leadership

2.3.1 Defining Cultural Intelligence/ Cultural Quotient (CQ)

It's imperative as an inclusive leader that you have an awareness of different cultures. Although you won't be able to remember everything about all cultures, an awareness that these differences exist and can impact people in different ways is very important. This knowledge is called cultural intelligence, or cultural quotient (CQ).

---

25. Saputra, Farhan. "Leadership, communication, and work motivation in determining the success of professional organizations." *Journal of Law, Politics and Humanities* 1, no. 2 (2021): 59-70.

When you have a strong sense of cultural intelligence, you understand differences and are adaptable when creating space for these differences. Demonstrating CQ goes beyond simply awareness of cultural diversity. Fully implementing CQ means you must be intentional about actively learning about other cultures, experiences, and norms to engage and communicate with diverse groups of people.

A strong sense of CQ can be something that is used inside and outside of the workplace. These skills will help you build strong and more effective relationships while managing conflict with more equity and empathy. However, building upon this competency will require that you have an open mind and motivation to grow more inclusive spaces based on the experiences and backgrounds of others. CQ is key to developing partnerships, understanding, and cohesiveness to increase access to opportunities for those of diverse and marginalized backgrounds.

2.3.2 CQ and inclusive leadership

CQ will be essential on your inclusive leadership journey. Leaders who have developed a high CQ have the ability to respond to cultural differences more effectively. There are several reasons why this is important not only for inclusive leaders, but for all leaders.[26]

- When you grow your cultural intelligence you have the opportunity to enhance your problem-solving skills. You will become equipped to address problems that may arise due to cultural diversity. You will also gain the perspective to notice barriers that may limit

---

26. Wang, Kenneth T., and Michael Goh. "Cultural intelligence." *The Wiley Encyclopedia of Personality and Individual Differences: Clinical, Applied, and Cross-Cultural Research* (2020): 269-273.

opportunity and impede growth and innovation processes.

- When you grow your cultural intelligence you have the opportunity to increase innovation as CQ gives teams the permission to be creative and take more risks. This will also provide different perspectives and viewpoints. This can lead to new ideas and products to gain market share.

- When you grow your cultural intelligence you are more prepared to address conflict. CQ is key in conflict resolution processes with people from diverse backgrounds. This will allow you to mediate conflict by understanding differences while ensuring equity and empathy.

- When you grow your cultural intelligence, you will develop a more global perspective. As society continues to evolve toward more diversity, it's important that leaders have a deep understanding of different cultures and how those impact the economy. This knowledge will provide insights to grow business and expand market share.

- When you grow your cultural intelligence, you also have the opportunity to grow personally. It will allow you to expand your horizons and evolve your perspective. You will also be able to decrease your biases and be more authentic in your inclusion work.

2.3.3 Equipping leaders with the right tools

As an inclusive leader on the journey to growing your CQ mindset, there are several options you can use. The most common way is through increasing your awareness through education and training. This will allow you to gain more knowledge about different cultures. This approach to learning can take many forms such as formal programming, workshops, online courses, and cultural events. You can also increase your cultural intelligence through engaging in less familiar activities that include people of diverse cultures. This can be done through traveling, working abroad, and attending meetings that address barriers for people of diverse backgrounds.

Most of all, it is important to have an open mind while being curious and respecting individual differences.

Chapter Summary

- Growing as an inclusive leader means learning about different cultures, traditions, and customs to develop a deeper understanding.
- Actively listening is key to learning about other cultures.
- Empathy to connect with team members on a personal level and appreciation of their unique backgrounds will be required for growth.
- Promoting open communication will lead to the sharing of diverse viewpoints and the creation of a safe space to share.
- As CQ increases, skills to resolve conflicts will increase which is essential for an inclusive leader.

Quiz

1. What are the traits of inclusive leadership?
   a. Empathy
   b. Fairness
   c. Open Communication
   d. All the above

2. Why is inclusion as a leadership trait important?
   a. It boosts employee morale
   b. Create an unsafe environment
   c. Doesn't promote productivity
   d. All the above

3. How can leaders grow mindsets around inclusion?
   a. Embrace Challenges
   b. Learn from Feedback
   c. Persist in the Face of Adversity
   d. All the above

4. What are the four main leadership styles in situational leadership?
   a. Directing
   b. Coaching
   c. Supporting
   d. All the above

5. Kim is a new leader and wants to know how to best support her team. You advise that leaders should be flexible and able to switch between different styles based on the situation and team. This dynamic is called:
   a. Adaptability
   b. Flexibility
   c. Respect
   d. Fairness

6. What is it called when you recognize your strengths and weaknesses to leverage what you excel in and improve the areas that need development?
   a. Inclusion
   b. Development
   c. Self-Awareness
   d. Communication

7. What is it called when you align personal values with your leadership approach?
   a. Authenticity and credibility
   b. Diversity
   c. Safety
   d. Leadership

8. When you have continuous growth and development, you are:
   a. Aware of your leadership style and identity
   b. Seek feedback
   c. Learn from experience and adapt to new challenges
   d. All the above

9. Why is delegating important for inclusive leadership?
   a. It empowers members to make decisions and take ownership of their work
   b. It creates fear in employees
   c. Some people lack motivation
   d. All the above

10. What can leaders do to recognize the needs of their team members and adapt their leadership style accordingly?
    a. Build strong relationships
    b. Enhance team performance
    c. Drive overall success within the organization
    d. All the above

Answers

1 – d	2 – a	3 – d	4 – d	5 – a
6 – c	7 – a	8 – d	9 – a	10 – d

Case Study

Revolutionizing Company Culture at GreenTech Industries

Overview

GreenTech Industries (name changed for privacy), is a mid-sized firm in the renewable energy sector. Kimbrel Management Consulting worked with the organization to discover a crucial gap in genuine inclusion despite having a diverse team, a challenge echoed by research.[27] Recognizing that this shortfall could impede both innovation [28] and employee contentment, GreenTech's leadership proactively engaged in strategies articulated in our consulting approach to cultivate a truly inclusive atmosphere.[29]

Strategy

1. **DEI audit:** We initiated a comprehensive internal assessment to scrutinize existing protocols and pinpoint areas primed for inclusivity advancements.[30]
2. **Leadership development:** We conducted specialized workshops to enhance leadership skills, focusing significantly on transformational and participative leadership methodologies.[31]
3. **Cultivating cultural intelligence:** We launched targeted training programs designed to equip employees

---

[27]. Dr. DeAnna Kimbrel-Hopkins, *Strategically Strengthen Your Leadership: Master DEI Challenges* (2025).

[28]. Amy C. Edmondson. *The Fearless Organization: Creating Psychological Safety in the Workplace for Learning, Innovation, and Growth.* Hoboken, NJ: Wiley, 2018.

[29]. Michael C. Hyter and Judith L. Turnock. *The Power of Inclusion: Unlock the Potential and Productivity of Your Workforce.* Hoboken, NJ: Wiley, 2020.

[30]. Iris Bohnet. *What Works: Gender Equality by Design.* Cambridge: Belknap Press, 2016.

[31]. Charlotte Sweeney and Fleur Bothwick. *Inclusive Leadership: The Definitive Guide to Developing and Executing an Impactful Diversity and Inclusion Strategy.* London: Financial Times Publishing, 2017.

with the competency to appreciate cultural diversity and enhance their abilities in cross-cultural communication.[32]

Impacts

- **Innovation surge:** By fostering an environment where more voices contribute, GreenTech experienced a remarkable 30% boost in new project initiatives.
- **Improved employee satisfaction:** Feedback from employee surveys revealed a 40% hike in workplace satisfaction and an increased sense of belonging, underscoring the effectiveness of our inclusive strategies.
- **Enhanced retention:** Employee engagement and perceived value led to a 20% improvement in retention rates, demonstrating the benefits of a supportive work culture.

Insightful takeaways

- **Value of continuous feedback:** Consistent feedback sessions proved indispensable in refining and advancing DEI strategies, highlighting their role in adaptive organizational growth.
- **Commitment at the top:** The commitment of a dedicated leadership team was pivotal in driving these efforts (De Aquino & Robertson, 2018)[33], illustrating the necessity of leadership engagement in successful initiative deployment.

Through these tailored consulting services, GreenTech Industries successfully transformed its workplace culture, showcasing the potent impact of strategic leadership development and inclusivity programs (Kimbrel-Hopkins, 2025).

---

32. Mahzarin Banaji and Anthony Greenwald. *Blindspot: Hidden Biases of Good People*. New York: Delacorte Press, 2013.

33. Carlos Tasso Eira de Aquino and Robert W. Robertson. *Diversity and Inclusion in the Global Workplace: Aligning Initiatives with Strategic Business Goals*. Cham: Springer, 2018.

Discussion questions

1. What critical hurdles might an organization encounter when striving to uncover gaps in inclusion across different hierarchical levels?
2. In conducting a DEI assessment, how can organizations gain profound insights into their prevailing inclusivity practices, and which focal points should command attention?
3. How can leadership development workshops that emphasize transformational and participative leadership techniques foster a culture of inclusivity and cooperation within an organization?
4. What advantages do employees derive from engaging in training initiatives designed to elevate cultural intelligence and the skills necessary for effective cross-cultural communication?
5. What methodologies can organizations employ to accurately gauge the impact of their inclusivity initiatives concerning innovation, employee morale, and workforce retention?
6. What strategic approaches can be applied to ensure the continuous collection and effective use of feedback for the refinement of DEI strategies?
7. Why is the involvement of the leadership team essential for the successful execution of DEI initiatives, and what measures can be taken to motivate leaders to take proactive roles?
8. How can the achievements of GreenTech Industries in reshaping its workplace culture serve as a catalyst for other organizations aspiring to elevate their inclusion practices?

CHAPTER 3
Power and Justice in Inclusive Leadership

Key Learning Objectives
- Power in the workplace
- Justice in the workplace
- Sphere of influence in the workplace
- Leadership and equity
- Workplace culture and leadership
- Cultivating a positive workplace culture

3.1 Power, Justice, and Influence

3.1.1 Power in the workplace

As an inclusive leader, it's important to understand the significance of societal power. It can have many meanings based on the context used. Often it is used to describe the capacity to do something that includes strength, control, influence, or authority over others. You will find many examples of power in every area of life such as personal relationships to social, business, and governmental circumstances. Power can yield positive results such as changes toward equity and inclusion while also having the ability to yield negative results such as marginalization and oppression. According to Figure 3.1, understanding the concept of power requires a nuanced perspective that considers its many dimensions and implications in society.

Figure 3.1 Types of workplace power

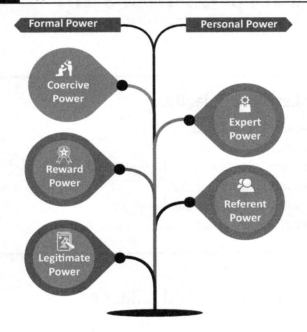

Source: *Expert Program Management.* "*Types of Workplace Power.*" Accessed January 18, 2025. http://www.expertprogrammanagement.com

Implementing power in the workplace

Power dynamics can play out in many different ways within an organizational structure including how employees communicate and build relationships.[34]

- Legitimate power is based on organizational roles, such as a manager or team leader.
- Expert power is acquired by what someone knows or their expertise.
- Referent power is developed based on likability, and the ability to influence others through personal connections.
- Coercive is influence based on control or coercion.

Having a clear understanding of these types of power can help you to guide the complex situations you will encounter in the workplace with people of diverse backgrounds. Power in the workplace can be used to inspire others to innovate and achieve organizational goals. Without a clear understanding, the application of power can decrease morale, impede productivity, and lead to toxic work environments. As an inclusive leader, you must be aware of power dynamics, promote fairness, and cultivate respect and collaboration. When there is a healthy balance of power and effective communication, a thriving organization with inclusivity is created.

3.1.2 Justice in the workplace

Justice is another important concept that must be understood and operationalized by you as an inclusive leader. Justice is often defined by a sense and structure of

---

34. Kovach, Mary. "Leader influence: A research review of French & Raven's (1959) power dynamics." *The Journal of Values-Based Leadership* 13, no. 2 (2020): 15.

fairness and equity. This is evident when people are treated in a way that is legally required and morally acceptable. This means that everyone, regardless of background, is treated without discrimination or bias. There are many forms of justice to consider, such as:[35]

- **Legal justice:** It is the most common concept related to justice. This refers to the administration of justice that is impartial and equal for all.
- **Social justice:** It is another form of justice that focuses on systemic inequalities and injustices that exist in society. It strives to ensure equal access to opportunities and rights for everyone, regardless of their background or circumstances.
- **Distributive justice:** It refers to the fair allocation of the tools and resources people need to thrive. The goal is to mitigate the disparities in wealth and essential services for those who are traditionally marginalized.

As you continue to evolve as an inclusive leader, you will play a pivotal role in implementing a structure for fairness, equality, and accountability. This includes the treatment of employees, compliance with anti-discrimination and workplace laws, and conflict resolution regardless of race, gender, or age. The essential features are pay equity, opportunity for advancements, and physical and psychological safety.

---

[35]. Fine, Cordelia, Victor Sojo, and Holly Lawford-Smith. "Why does workplace gender diversity matter? Justice, organizational benefits, and policy." *Social Issues and Policy Review* 14, no. 1 (2020): 36-72.

In your role within the organization, you may also be responsible for managing grievances or conflicts. This is an essential process that requires transparent procedures, proper addressal of concerns and disputes, and a platform for team members to be heard and understood. Through ensuring a culture of justice, workplace environments will grow around inclusion and equity in a way that is tangible for all employees.

Implementing justice in the workplace

Establishing a culture of accountability and transparency:

- Implementing policies to promote truth-telling and the sharing of adverse experiences and processes to report incidents without fear will create a culture of transparency. An example of this is a whistleblower policy[36]
- Conducting regular reviews of policies and procedures to ensure they are being properly implemented will provide accountability for the changes you are seeking

Providing ongoing training and education:

- Offering workshops and training on topics like unconscious bias, cultural awareness, and conflict resolution can help team members understand and address DEI-related issues
- Providing information on DEI support at the start of the employee journey at onboarding will contribute to equitable and inclusive workplaces

---

36. Kang, Minsung Michael. "Whistleblowing in the public sector: a Systematic literature review." *Review of Public Personnel Administration* 43, no. 2 (2023): 381-406.

Fostering a sense of community and support:

- Creating environments and activities that help team members develop a sense of community will increase belonging
- Implementing structures like employee resource groups or affinity groups can help create support for team members of different backgrounds

Measuring and monitoring progress:

- Maintaining a pulse on the workforce through regular feedback mechanisms like surveys and forums will allow you to gauge employee experiences with justice and fairness in your work environment
- Creating effective performance measures to assess the impact of DEI practices within the organization will allow your progress and where contingencies need to be implemented

Celebrating and recognizing diversity:

- Internationally bringing awareness to other cultures and celebrating differences will help team members develop purpose within the organization and feel seen
- Sharing personal stories, traditions, and cultures will promote diversity and create a common understanding among team members

3.1.3 Sphere of influence in the workplace

Inclusive leadership also relies on the power of influence. It refers to the ability to impact the character, growth, or actions of individuals or things. According to Figure 3.2, this includes the authority to mold beliefs, motivate behaviors, or affect choices. Influence can originate from different origins like individuals, institutions, media, or societal standards, and it has a substantial impact on shaping connections, culture, and society.

Figure 3.2   Sphere of influence

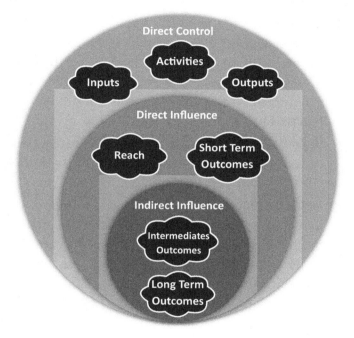

Source: *Minutetools. 7 Dec. 2022, https://expertprogrammanagement.com/*

As an inclusive leader, it's important to recognize the concept of influence as it helps with understanding how ideas and decisions are made. Influence manifests in many areas of life, such as:

- **Types of influence:**

- **Direct influence:** This occurs when there is a clear and immediate impact on others' behavior and decision-making. For example, a leader's influence on a team's approach to work.
- **Indirect influence:** This involves a subtle approach to changing the attitudes and behaviors of people over time.

- **Sources of influence:**
  - **Status influences:** People can be influenced by the status of people such as leaders, celebrities, or experts. Based on status people can hold a significant influence over others and their behaviors.
  - **Organizational influences:** Entities like organizations or companies can influence people through their cultures, policies, and practices.
  - **Media influence:** The media can also influence people and shape public opinions. For example, mass media outlets like TV and social media can play an essential role in forming how people think and influencing societal trends.
  - **Societal norms:** Cultural traditions can also play a big role in how people think and influence their decision-making processes.

- **Impact of influence:**
  - **Shaping behavior:** This happens when people are guided toward a particular action or behavior that will impact professional and social behaviors and decisions.

- **Inspiring change:** This happens when people are positively influenced to make a change or progress.
- **Building relationships:** This happens when people build networks and relationships that impact decisions and behaviors.

As an inclusive leader, when you are able to understand what motivates people, you will be able to tailor your tactics to influencing change. Some effective ways to do this can be displaying empathy, building relationships, and collaboration. The ability to positively influence is also imperative in inspiring others. When you can properly influence others you will be able to properly communicate visions, purpose, and justice. When people feel respected and included, they are more likely to thrive. Employees feel appreciated, engaged, and driven to excel.[37]

3.2 Leadership and Equity

3.2.1 Equity vs. equality

As an inclusive leader, it is important to understand the difference between equity and equality. Oftentimes people use these terms interchangeably, however, they have different and important meanings. According to Figure 3.3, equality refers to the traditional notion of fairness in that everyone receives the same resources, opportunities, and treatment regardless of their differences. On the other hand, equity stands on the basis that each person has unique needs and required resources and opportunities to be successful.

---

37. Allas, Tera, and Bill Schaninger. "The boss factor: Making the world a better place through workplace relationships." *The McKinsey Quarterly* (2020).

Figure 3.3 Equity vs Equality

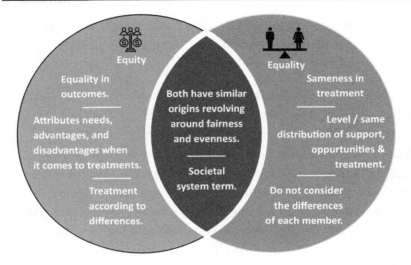

Source: *"Equality vs Equity: Unravelling the Distinctions."* https://www.linkedin.com

An important role as an inclusive leader is advocacy for human rights. This largely includes being a voice around fairness. This requires speaking up for equitable practices over equality mindsets. When equity is prioritized within an organization, organizations can authentically develop more inclusive environments where all team members have access to opportunity. This approach will allow you to cultivate more productivity and justice within your workplace.[38]

3.2.2 Leadership and equity

As an inclusive leader, promoting equity will allow you to combat systemic issues related to DEI and discrimination, developing an inclusive and diverse workplace. Empowering team members through equity can lead to increased morale,

---

38. Livingston, Robert. "How to promote racial equity in the workplace." *Harvard Business Review* 98, no. 5 (2020): 64-72.

productivity, and creativity. Additionally, equitable leadership will attract top talent, since team members will feel valued and respected.[39]

Beyond the workplace, advocating for equity contributes to a more just society. Role modeling, inclusive practices, and challenging systemic inequalities are what will drive social change. This mindset will transcend communities and foster resilience and growth. An authentic commitment to equity will enable leaders to have a profound impact on the world.

3.2.3 Implementing equity in the workplace

As an inclusive leader, it's important to understand the key elements of equity which include a particular regard for fairness, access to opportunity, and respect. When you are able to prioritize equity, you will be able to properly leverage the benefits of having a diverse team.

The benefits of diversity include innovation, different perspectives, and a more just and productive work environment. When team members have clear evidence of fairness, they will be more likely to bring their full selves to the organization and work at their highest level. Producing equitable work environments isn't just the right thing to do, it is also a business strategy. Below are ways to promote equity in work environments:

- **Creating Employee Resource Groups (ERGs):** A platform for team members to come together, share experiences, and bring awareness and insights into the organizational culture.

---

39. Bohonos, J.W. and Sisco, S., 2021. Advocating for social justice, equity, and inclusion in the workplace: An agenda for anti-racist learning organizations. *New Directions for Adult and Continuing Education, 2021*(170), pp.89-98.

- **Assessing the cultural climate:** This can be done with regular DEI and climate surveys to gather feedback on experiences and track key trends.
- **Adding visibility to the contributions:** Making the contributions of team members from marginalized backgrounds visible through events or awards can help develop a sense of belonging in the workplace.
- **Implementing anti-discrimination policies and governance processes:** Such processes outline procedures to prohibit discrimination and harassment, along with adequate reporting strategies, thus creating safe spaces and inclusivity for all team members.

These strategies are imperative for an inclusive leader as they will assist with fostering a culture where inclusion and equity are tangible and all employees feel respected, valued, and empowered to thrive.

3.3 Workplace Culture and Leadership

3.3.1 Workplace culture

Understanding the nuances of an inclusive workplace culture will be imperative in your role as an inclusive leader. Workplace culture can be defined as the values, beliefs, and attitudes shared between team members in a particular work environment. Workplace cultures often consist of unwritten rules and norms that guide how team members engage.

When workplace cultures are positive, team members are more likely to develop a sense of belonging, which leads to increases in employee engagement, satisfaction, and productivity. Negative workplace cultures often yield high turnover rates, low engagement, and decreased performance.

As an inclusive leader, you address workplace culture through efforts related to leadership styles, communication practices, work environment, and company values. When organizations are authentic and intentional about their workplace culture, there is more opportunity for cohesiveness and overall success.

When it comes to workplace culture, the dynamics and atmosphere can significantly influence employee morale and productivity. Here are some key points to consider about different types of workplace cultures:[40]

- **Hierarchical culture:**
    - Clear chain of command
    - Top-down decision-making
    - Can lead to efficient decision-making
    - May stifle creativity and innovation at lower levels
- **Collaborative culture:**
    - Emphasis on teamwork
    - Open communication
    - Shared decision-making
    - Fosters a sense of unity and camaraderie among employees
    - Encourages creativity and diverse perspectives
- **Competitive culture:**
    - Focus on individual success and achievement
    - Drives employees to perform at their best
    - Can create a cut-throat environment
    - May lead to lack of collaboration and teamwork

---

40. Bodker, Keld, and Jesper Strandgaard Pedersen. "Workplace cultures: Looking at artifacts, symbols and practices." In *Design at work*, pp. 121-136. CRC Press, 2020.

- **Innovative culture:**
  - Prioritizes creativity and risk-taking
  - Encourages experimentation and out-of-the-box thinking
  - Can lead to breakthrough ideas and advancements
  - Requires a high tolerance for failure
- **Customer-centric culture:**
  - Focus on meeting customer needs and expectations
  - Drives customer satisfaction and loyalty
  - Encourages a strong customer service orientation
  - Requires employees to be responsive and adaptable to changing customer demands

3.3.2 Aligning values and goals

Working with your organization to create a culture that aligns with those within the workplace will require a keen understanding of differences and how people of diverse backgrounds may be impacted by organizational culture and values. When you intentionally seek out people from various backgrounds to join your team, you will be able to make informed decisions about how to shape your work environment for more inclusion and equity.[41]

As an inclusive leader, you can develop your workplace culture based on various values and sets of behaviors to engage within the organization. This shaping starts with leadership. Leaders are the change agents that shape the culture and climate within organizations. Leaders influence

---

41. Munir, Misbachul, and Samsul Arifin. "Organizational Culture and Impact on Improving Employee Performance." *Journal of Social Science Studies (JOS3)* 1, no. 2 (2021): 65-68.

culture through communication, decision-making, and attitude

Team members also largely contribute to the culture of an organization. Each employee brings a different perspective that is reflective of their experiences, work styles, backgrounds, and norms. All these factors contribute to how people engage in the workplace culture. Using these differences to influence the overall workplace culture will be imperative.

This can be achieved through implementing diverse hiring procedures, more awareness training for employees, and recognizing different cultures. Organizations also play an important role in shaping a diverse and inclusive culture by creating space for people to share experiences, policies to hold people accountable for changes, and providing the resources to implement the changes they would like to see.

3.3.3 Toxic work cultures

As an inclusive leader, you must be aware of the toxicity that may exist within your workplace and/or on your team. A toxic culture can be rooted in many different things like poor leadership, a lack of inclusion and equity, and a lack of communication. Toxic work cultures can lead to a lack of engagement and resiliency among team members. It can also lead to turnover and low productivity.

Bullying and harassment may contribute to toxic workplace cultures. Harassment can happen in many different ways such as verbal, physical, and emotional. Oftentimes this is called a hostile work environment. This creates threats to psychological safety and productivity. Additionally, toxicity in the workplace can be attributed to the presence of biases and inequalities creating spaces where people feel marginalized or alienated.[42]

Toxicity in workplaces can also be from working conditions such as demanding work and unrealistic goals. These things can lead to a lack of engagement, efficacy, and morale. These culture killers can be addressed by improving communication, leadership practices, goal setting, and fostering a culture where team members feel included and respected. Leadership plays an important role here as leaders are responsible for identifying toxicity, not perpetuating it, and eliminating or reducing harm. When a toxic work culture is not addressed by leaders, it can be perpetuated, which can impact the overall climate of the organization.

Good leaders can cure toxic cultures by setting positive examples and being good communicators who are authentic and empathetic. Leaders should also practice effective conflict resolution tactics that reflect equity and fairness. These actions will help leaders hold themselves and others responsible for their actions, and actively work toward building a culture of equity and inclusion.

Workplace culture is a very critical piece of a thriving organization as it shapes the way people communicate, behave, and interact with each other. It is something that will continue to evolve as people and society evolve. It is also something that must be consistently measured and addressed. This will lead to an increase in morale, collaboration, communication, and overall productivity.

---

42. Abbas, Muzaffar, and Ghazi Ben Saad. "An empirical investigation of toxic leadership traits impacts on workplace climate and harassment." *Talent Development & Excellence* 12, no. 3 (2020): 2317-2333.

3.3.4 Effectively leading through workplace culture

The culture of your work environment will be a very important factor in your role as an inclusive leader. When you are able to cultivate a positive culture you will be able to foster increased employee engagement, productivity, and retention. As a leader that focuses on positive workplaces, you will be able to motivate your teams and gain trust.

Additionally, the culture of the work environment will influence decision-making, conflict resolution, and communication. By nurturing a positive work culture, you will create cohesive teams that will work in alignment. A positive culture can also be used to attract potential candidates and help with branding. When team members experience a positive culture, they are likely to share those experiences with others.

3.3.5 Fostering a positive culture

Although your role as an inclusive leader is imperative to cultivating work environments where everyone thrives, organizations are vital to real change. The values of the organization will guide sustainable change within an organization. These values are the overall foundation for the culture and will determine how individuals within the organization interact internally and externally. Often, organizational values can be centered around integrity, respect, teamwork, innovation, customer focus, and social responsibility. The values of the organization will guide the team through difficult times and times of uncertainty.

It's also important to ensure employees feel seen and heard. This can be done through recognition programs and options for a healthy work-life balance. Investing in your team's development and well-being will contribute to a culture of belonging and inclusion. In practice this can look like[43]:

- Professional development and training
- Flexibility in work hours or remote work options
- Team-building activities and social events
- Wellness programs or initiatives, such as mental health resources or fitness challenges
- Open communication and feedback

---

43. Bhat, Meghana Moorthy, Saghar Hosseini, Ahmed Hassan, Paul Bennett, and Weisheng Li. "Say 'YES' to positivity: Detecting toxic language in workplace communications." In *Findings of the Association for Computational Linguistics: EMNLP 2021*, pp. 2017-2029. 2021.

Chapter Summary

- As an inclusive leader, it's important to understand the significance of societal power. It can have many meanings based on the context used. Often it is used to describe the capacity to do something that includes strength, control, influence, or authority over others.

- Justice is another important concept that must be understood and operationalized by you as an inclusive leader. Justice is often defined by a sense and structure of fairness and equity. This is evident when people are treated in a way that is legally required and morally acceptable.

- As you continue to evolve as an inclusive leader, you will play a pivotal role in implementing a structure for fairness, equality, and accountability. This includes the treatment of employees, compliance with anti-discrimination and workplace laws, and conflict resolution regardless of race, gender, or age.

- As an inclusive leader, it's important to recognize the concept of influence as it helps with understanding how ideas and decisions are made.

- Equity stands on the basis that each person has unique needs and required resources and opportunities to be successful.

- As an inclusive leader, it's important to understand the key elements of equity, which include a particular regard for fairness, access to opportunity, and respect. When you can prioritize equity, you will be able to properly leverage the benefits of having a diverse team.

- Workplace culture can be defined as the values, beliefs, and attitudes shared between team members in a particular work environment. Workplace cultures often consist of unwritten rules and norms that guide how team members engage.
- A toxic culture can be rooted in many different things like poor leadership, a lack of inclusion, a lack of equity, and a lack of communication. Toxic work cultures can lead to a lack of engagement and resiliency among team members. It can also lead to turnover and low productivity.

Quiz

1. **Power dynamics can exist within an organization and are categorized as:**
   a. Legitimate power comes from a person's title within an organizational structure, such as a manager or team leader.
   b. Expert power is developed through a leader's knowledge, skills, and expertise in a particular field or subject matter.
   c. Referent power comes from a person's charisma, likability, and ability to influence others through personal connections.
   d. All the above

2. **Justice can be defined as the principle of fairness and equity. In which form of justice are these qualities not visible?**
   a. Legal justice
   b. Social justice
   c. Distributive justice
   d. None of the above

3. **Inclusive leadership also relies on the power of influence, which refers to:**
   a. The ability to impact the character, growth, or actions of individuals or things
   b. Creating a hostile working environment
   c. Not giving people the ability to communicate
   d. All of the above

4. Sources of Influence include:
   a. Individuals
   b. Organizations
   c. Media
   d. All the above

5. Leadership power empowers individuals to do all but:
   a. Make decisions
   b. Assign responsibilities
   c. Impose cultural beliefs
   d. None of the above

6. While equality focuses on treating everyone the same, equity centers on:
   a. Making group decisions on the majority
   b. Addressing individual needs and offering support where it is most needed.
   c. Intention in creating plans
   d. All of the above

7. Leaders who emphasize equity strive to create an environment where everyone has:
   a. Equal access to opportunities
   b. Lack of a sense of belonging
   c. Assistance
   d. All the above

8. A positive workplace culture fosters:
   a. High morale
   b. Decreased performance
   c. Increase turnover
   d. None of the above

9. A negative culture can lead to:
   a. Employee engagement
   b. Satisfaction
   c. High Turnover
   d. None of the Above

10. By advancing equity, leaders can combat:
    a. Systemic biases
    b. Discrimination
    c. Lack of inclusive and diverse workplace
    d. All the above

Answers

1 – d	2 – d	3 – a	4 – d	5 – d
6 – b	7 – d	8 – a	9 – c	10 – d

Chapter 4
Inclusion as a Leadership Strategy

Key Learning Objectives
- Strategic inclusion and becoming an inclusive leader
- Empowering teams through inclusive leadership
- Culturally centered communication
- Understanding communication styles
- Systemically leveraging cultural differences

Chapter Four covers the key concepts of inclusive leadership. Inclusive leadership refers to a leader's ability to create diverse and inclusive work environments that thrive by implementing equitable practices. Some of the key characteristics associated with inclusive leaders are cultivating a supportive and welcoming environment, listening to different viewpoints, promoting equality, and embracing diversity.

4.1 Strategic Inclusion: Communication Across Cultural Differences

4.1.1 Becoming an inclusive leader

Becoming an inclusive leader and building cohesive teams require more than just words; it involves taking concrete actions to foster an environment where everyone can thrive.[44] Some key strategies for implementing inclusive leadership strategies are:

- Creating a space where team members feel safe having difficult conversations
- Embracing different perspectives and ideas in decision-making processes
- Ensuring all team members have the tools and resources needed to grow and develop according to individual needs
- Addressing biases that may impact the team's ability to work effectively and inclusively
- Embracing and recognizing cultural differences and norms
- Creating policies that keep teams accountable for changes around DEI within the workplace

---

44. Roberson, Quinetta, and Jamie L. Perry. "Inclusive leadership in thought and action: A thematic analysis." *Group & Organization Management* 47, no. 4 (2022): 755-778.

4.1.2 The six C's of inclusive leadership

Figure 4.1 Six signature traits of an inclusive leader

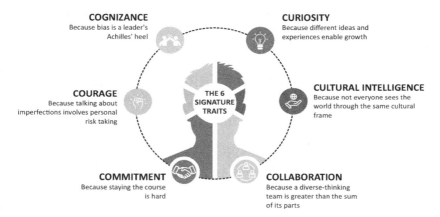

Source: *"Inclusive Leadership and Why It Matters." Qualtrics,* https://www.qualtrics.com/experience-management/employee/inclusive-leadership/.

According to Figure 4.1, the following are the six traits of an inclusive leader:

A. **Cognizance:** Highly inclusive leaders are aware of cultural differences and how biases impact decisions and actions.

B. **Cultural intelligence:** Highly inclusive leaders demonstrate cultural efficacy in their behaviors while ensuring fairness and equality in all interactions.

C. **Commitment:** Highly inclusive leaders are enabled to effectively convey their commitment to diversity and inclusion.

D. **Courage:** Highly inclusive leaders demonstrate courage when advocating for DEI.

E. **Curiosity:** Highly inclusive leaders are continuous learners and are open to new opportunities to grow their knowledge around diversity and inclusion.
F. **Collaboration:** Highly inclusive leaders work collaboratively to embrace different cultures and recognize the unique strengths of their team members and within the organization.

4.2 Communication and Cultural Inclusion

4.2.1 Culturally centered communication

Inclusive leaders work to ensure that all team members are empowered to put forth maximum effort in their work. When leaders are intentional about creating safe work environments with a sense of trust and inclusion, team members are more likely to reach the common goals of the team and organization. Through the efforts of inclusive leadership, creativity, and innovation, team performance can grow. It's also key to remember that inclusive leadership is not just about tolerance, but about actively embracing and celebrating differences to create a more equitable and productive work environment. One key trait of an effective inclusive leader is communication.[45] Below are tips for effective communication across different cultures:

- **Active listening:** Being an inclusive leader means actively listening to team members, creating safe spaces for team members to bring their full selves to the work environment, and offering feedback to promote a culture of respect and understanding.

---

45. Roberson, Quinetta, and Jamie L. Perry. "Inclusive leadership in thought and action: A thematic analysis." *Group & Organization Management* 47, no. 4 (2022): 755-778.

- **Being transparent:** As an inclusive leader, you should be clear about goals and expectations and ensure everyone is working toward common goals.
- **Giving clear cues:** You must ensure your verbal and nonverbal cues convey inclusivity and trust-building.
- **Active engagement:** You must also actively engage in meetings, discussions, and opportunities to informally communicate with your team which can lead to stronger team cohesion.
- **Being intentional:** You must be intentional about clearly setting priorities. Developing and communicating priorities will allow you to create a work environment where everyone thrives and understands the organizational direction.

Effective communication plays an important role in cultivating an equitable and inclusive environment. Communication is a tool that can be used to transmit information as well as build relationships, understand differences, and create opportunities for growth for all.

As a leader, it is your responsibility to be aware of different communication styles, norms, and languages that can exist within a diverse, ever-changing workforce, and create strategies to ensure everyone feels valued and welcomed.[46] Figure 4.2, demonstrates the many layers of DEI that leaders must be aware of in order to effectively communicate across cultural differences.

---

46. Gist-Mackey, A. N., & Kingsford, A. N. (2020). Linguistic inclusion: Challenging implicit classed communication bias in interview methods. *Management Communication Quarterly, 34*(3), 402-425.

Figure 4.2 Belonging: A conversation about equity, diversity and inclusion source

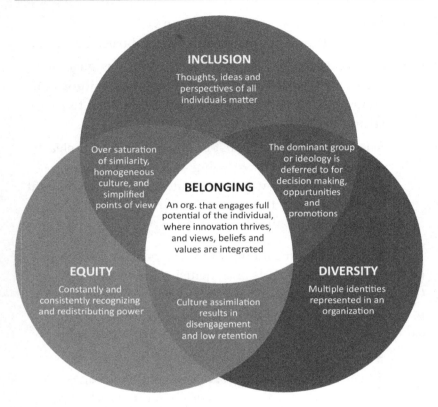

Source: *Krys Burnette. "Belonging: A Conversation about Equity, Diversity & Inclusion." Accessed March 8, 2025. https://www.krysburnette.com*

Cultural communication includes a broad range of methods through which culture can be expressed, ideas can be shared, and understanding can be fostered. These different communication forms are foundational to how societies construct identities, navigate differences, and build connections across diverse communities. Communication can be categorized across cultures according to verbal, nonverbal, and/or symbolic which have different meanings and significance.

Verbal communication varies within and outside of cultures and includes different languages, dialects, and accents, which are most often characteristic of cultural expression. These language differences are used to help people communicate casually and formally in day-to-day life as well as to narrate historical accounts, convey cultural norms, and capture memories. Activities like oratory storytelling and proverbs help to communicate traditions and customs. Also, the tone, rate, and pitch of language can be used to convey emotions while communicating, which can also vary vastly among different cultural groups[47].

Outside of what people say, it's how they say it. This is considered non-verbal communication and includes a wide variety of actions and practices that communicate meaning without language. For example, facial gestures and eye contact can communicate respect or a lack thereof based on different cultures and can cause conflict without any words.

As an inclusive leader, it is imperative to understand the significance of different cultures and languages – verbal and nonverbal. Also, consider the use of space and how it can be used to communicate nonverbally, such as cultural norms surrounding social distance and interactions. As a leader, it is also important to consider cultural differences when it comes to attire, colors, and hairstyles.

Symbols are also important forms of communication that leaders must be aware of when leading diverse teams. This can include art, music, and ceremonies that communicate cultural norms. Cultural symbols can be deeply rooted in the overall identity, shared beliefs, and history of a particular

---

[47]. Holliday, Adrian. "Culture, communication, context, and power." *The Routledge handbook of language and intercultural communication* (2020): 39-54.

culture. These shared norms create a common language that can transcend barriers of language. Shared symbols can act as change agents to express collective values, mark significant life events, and establish social bonds across cultures.

These different communication forms are imperative to understanding the role culture plays in communicating as a leader. Communication is the fabric that holds different communities together and is the key to understanding important differences between people from diverse backgrounds. Understanding communication will allow you to build better relationships, increase empathy, and build bridges across diverse cultures.

4.2.2 Understanding communication styles

In your role as an inclusive leader, it is also important to understand the different styles of communication among your team members. The way that people communicate can vary based on experiences and cultural background. When you have an awareness that communication styles will differ among team members, and know how to address these differences, you will be able to build a more equitable and inclusive team and working environment.[48]

Traditionally, communication styles can be broken down into 4 main categories – passive, assertive, passive-aggressive, and aggressive.

- Passiveness is when communication lacks true feelings regarding a situation.
- Assertiveness is when communication is open, and true thoughts and feelings are expressed while also

---

48. Raslie, Humaira. "Gen Y and gen Z communication style." Studies of Applied Economics 39, no. 1 (2021).

showing respect to others. This is often the preferred and most effective style of communication as it promotes clarity and mutual respect.

- Passive-aggressiveness is when communication is indirect. However, people appear to be passive on the surface but their actions display aggression in subtle ways, like sarcasm or backhanded compliments.
- Aggressiveness is when communication displays true thoughts and feelings in a disrespectful and forceful manner. This style is less effective because it disregards the needs of others.

When you can properly manage diverse communication styles, you are able to fully engage team members of different backgrounds and cultures. Additionally, being aware of your own communication style and how it is influenced by your experiences and culture increases your ability to learn more and adapt to other styles of communicating.

4.2.3 Effectively adopting communication styles

One of the most valuable tools in your inclusion leadership toolkit is effective communication. As discussed above, your ability to tailor your approach to communication among diverse groups will allow you to create more inclusive work environments.[49] Below are some tips to improve your communication:

---

49. Musheke, Mukelabai M., and Jackson Phiri. "The effects of effective communication on organizational performance based on the systems theory." *Open Journal of Business and Management* 9, no. 2 (2021): 659-671.

1. **Determine your natural communication style and preferences:** Recognizing your communication style and its roots will allow you to understand how they are impacting your leadership abilities. To effectively adapt to diverse leadership styles, a leader must be self-aware. It's also important to determine your own communication preferences. Do you like communication that is more or less direct? Is verbal or written communication most effective for you? Which symbols are most significant to you?

2. **Ensure your communication style fits your audience:** Your communication style matters as diverse groups can receive and understand information in a variety of ways. For example, some people may require a more direct approach while others might respond better to a less direct approach. Having general knowledge of different communication styles will give you an idea of how to tailor your message based on the demographics of your group.

3. **Determine the best channels to communicate:** There are many ways to convey messages to an audience which can be more or less traditional from face-to-face communication to virtual methods such as teleconferencing or via social media. As a leader, you must be aware of the options and technologies that are available to help deliver and/or amplify your messages. For example, virtual publications may be effective for getting information to large groups at once whereas one-on-one communication may be a better option to address individual issues with team members.

4. **Develop feedback loops:** Ensuring that you are able to receive and give feedback is essential to your development and those you lead. You can receive feedback in several ways, from formal to informal feedback methods, such as direct communication, surveys, and other assessments. This will help you grow as a leader and make more equitable decisions.

4.3 Systemically Leveraging Cultural Differences

4.3.1 Managing cultural influence

The differences that exist within teams can be impactful in organizational structures, engagement, and decision-making. Different cultures can bring about differences in concepts of teams and goals whereas some may focus more on relationship building while others are more focused on assertiveness and achievements. If these differences are not properly addressed they can lead to conflict over styles of leadership, teamwork, and resolving conflict. It's also important to consider and be aware of the impact of cultural norms on work-life balance, time management, and authority. As an inclusive leader, these components will allow you to be authentic in creating work environments that truly offer everyone the opportunity to thrive. In Figure 4.3, there are several cultural identities that must be considered when leaders are seeking to understand the differences that exist in their teams. Although it is impossible to know everything about all cultures, the key is to remember there are differences and be curious about identifying them and addressing them as a leadership practice.

| Figure 4.3 | Understanding Cultural Identities |

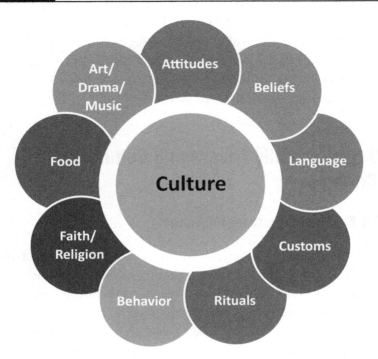

Source: *"Cultural Concept Diagram"*, https://www.cleanpng.com

4.3.2 Managing cultural conflicts

Often a lack of understanding and communication leads to conflict among groups of people of diverse backgrounds. When people of different backgrounds form a team, conflict is inevitable and often arises from diversity in beliefs, attitudes, backgrounds, and experiences. Cultural conflict can be blatant or very subtle. Cultural conflict can manifest in breakdowns in communication, relationship building, performance, and productivity. As an inclusive leader, it is important to understand the kind of conflicts that can arise, such as:

A. **Communication barriers:** Language differences are the most significant way that conflict can arise. Since language is derived from culture, when there is a lack of understanding of verbal and non-verbal cues can create barriers that impede the communication process. Some words, tones, or gestures can be viewed as disrespectful, rude, or aggressive, although that may not be the intent. These breakdowns in communication can lead to a build-up of animosity which may make it hard for team members to communicate and even work together.

B. **Differences in values and work style:** Differences in work ethics and generational styles of work can also be a prevalent cause of conflict in the workplace. Team members can have diverse thoughts regarding timelines, deadlines, autonomy, and flexibility. Additionally, there may be differences in how to address and challenge those positions of power (i.e. managers and superiors). Some may see assertiveness as insubordinate whereas others may feel that using your voice is the best option. Concepts surrounding work-life balance, teamwork, solo projects, hard vs smart work, and problem-solving techniques may also cause contention in work environments.

As an inclusive leader, your awareness of these barriers is imperative. Addressing them through open communication, learning diverse perspectives, and being flexible in your approach will help you be successful.

4.3.3 Managing cultural dynamics

It is your responsibility as an inclusive leader to address cultural differences on your team or within your organization that may cause conflict. It is very important that you are intentional about creating strategies to proactively address these issues. This can be very challenging and may require collaboration with other leaders to properly implement strategies to bring awareness to diversity, equity, and inclusion. Leaders and organizations start this process by acknowledging different cultural holidays, making space for cultural and religious practices, and changing or creating new policies that promote adherence to diverse communication, learning, and work styles like flexibility, work arrangements, and cultural sensitivity.[50]

However, something more important than all the practices discussed is that inclusive leaders are the role models for the changes they want to see. Although there is no end point of evolving around DEI, having the courage to demonstrate and advocate for inclusivity and diversity is the most effective tool for creating real change. These behaviors set the tone for the organization.

---

50. Mor Barak, Michàlle E., Gil Luria, and Kim C. Brimhall. "What leaders say versus what they do: Inclusive leadership, policy-practice decoupling, and the anomaly of climate for inclusion." *Group & Organization Management* 47, no. 4 (2022): 840-871.

Chapter Summary

- Becoming an inclusive leader and building cohesive teams require more than just words; it involves taking concrete actions to foster an environment where everyone can thrive
- When leaders are intentional about creating safe work environments with a sense of trust and inclusion, team members are more likely to work towards the common goals of the team and organization.
- Effective communication plays an important role in cultivating an equitable and inclusive environment. Communication is a tool that can be used to transmit information as well as build relationships, understand differences, and create opportunities for growth for all.
- Cultural communication includes a broad range of methods through which culture can be expressed, ideas shared, and understanding fostered.
- The differences that exist within teams can be impactful in organizational structures, engagement, and decision-making.
- Different cultures can bring about differences in the concepts of teams and goals – some may focus more on relationship building while others are more focused on assertiveness and achievements.
- It is your responsibility as an inclusive leader to address cultural differences on your team or within your organization that may cause conflict. It is very important that you are intentional about creating strategies to proactively address these issues.

Quiz

1. Key traits of inclusive leaders include:
   a. Addressing and mitigating bias
   b. Encouraging transparent communication
   c. Facilitating personal and professional growth
   d. All the above

2. Communication skills are crucial for an inclusive leader because:
   a. Effective leaders articulate their commitment to diversity and inclusion clearly to stakeholders.
   b. They increase misunderstandings and absenteeism through clear communication.
   c. They void ethical and transparent information sharing.
   d. All the above

3. Celebration of differences is important because:
   a. It doesn't highlight the organization's dedication to consistent communication across platforms, ensuring all members feel informed and included.
   b. It lacks the tools and strategies to enhance team engagement, promoting active participation and interaction.
   c. It values diverse backgrounds and experiences, leveraging these strengths to improve team dynamics and drive success.
   d. None of the above

4. **Key strategies for effective communication across different cultures include:**
   a. Being an active listener to grasp diverse viewpoints
   b. Ensuring transparency to build trust
   c. Utilizing non-verbal cues to enhance understanding
   d. All the above

5. **Communication is not just about transmitting information, but also about building relationships, understanding different perspectives, and creating a sense of belonging for all team members. A sense of belonging is:**
   a. When individuals are not present together meaningfully
   b. When communication is ineffective and non-inclusive
   c. An environment where individuals can express their true selves
   d. None of the above

6. **Verbal communication includes:**
   a. Languages, dialects, and accents to express ideas clearly
   b. Use of sign language for inclusive communication
   c. Written communication for clarity and record
   d. None of the above

7. **Non-verbal communication includes:**
   a. Body language
   b. Verbal cues
   c. International accents
   d. None of the above

8. Symbolic forms of communication include:
   a. Art, as a visual representation of ideas
   b. Music, to express emotions and cultural messages
   c. Rituals, embodying collective values and traditions
   d. All of the above

9. The primary communication styles are often categorized as:
   a. Assertive for clear and direct communication
   b. Passive as a non-confrontational approach
   c. Aggressive for forceful expression
   d. All of the above

10. Diversifying communication styles include:
    a. Tailoring your communication style to your audience for effectiveness
    b. Avoiding changing the pitch of your voice according to emotion
    c. Avoid increasing the speed of your communication because of excitement
    d. None of the Above

Answers

1 – d	2 – a	3 – c	4 – d	5 – c
6 – a	7 – a	8 – d	9 – d	10 – a

Case Study 2
Advancing DEI at Horizon Health Services

Introduction

Horizon Health Services (name changed for privacy), a prominent provider in the healthcare field, realized the necessity of weaving Diversity, Equity, and Inclusion (DEI) principles into its organizational framework.[51] This strategic move aimed at more effectively meeting the needs of a diverse patient population and fortifying team dynamics.[52] As demographic shifts broadened the spectrum of the community they serve, Horizon identified the limitations of a one-size-fits-all healthcare model, thus initiating steps toward fostering an inclusive and equitable ecosystem.[53]

Strategy overview

1. **Strategic visioning:** The leadership at Horizon embarked on an exhaustive review of its mission and organizational values to identify opportunities for seamlessly integrating DEI principles.[54] This comprehensive strategy not only defined precise goals but also outlined the stakeholders involved, establishing a roadmap for DEI milestones within a structured timeline. The goal was to ensure that

---

51. Carlos Tasso Eira de Aquino and Robert W. Robertson. *Diversity and Inclusion in the Global Workplace: Aligning Initiatives with Strategic Business Goals.* Cham: Springer, 2018.

52. Brené Brown. *Dare to Lead: Brave Work. Tough Conversations. Whole Hearts.* New York: Random House, 2019.

53. Mahzarin Banaji and Anthony Greenwald. *Blindspot: Hidden Biases of Good People.* New York: Delacorte Press, 2013.

54. Charlotte Sweeney and Fleur Bothwick. *Inclusive Leadership: The Definitive Guide to Developing and Executing an Impactful Diversity and Inclusion Strategy.* London: Financial Times Publishing, 2017.

DEI was reflected cohesively across all tiers of the organization.[55]

2. **Leadership engagement platforms:** Establishing leadership engagement platforms was crucial to Horizon's DEI initiatives. These forums functioned as interactive arenas where leaders discussed, shared insights, and tackled challenges related to inclusion.[56] The sessions were enriched with workshops, expert speakers, and collaborative roundtable dialogues, specifically aimed at imparting actionable strategies for integrating DEI across leadership strata and fostering a continuous culture of learning and dialogue.[57]

3. **Technological integration:** By integrating advanced analytics tools, Horizon meticulously tracked its DEI progress. These technological solutions were pivotal in providing precise evaluations of performance indicators, such as diversity metrics, patient feedback, and staff engagement. Utilizing business intelligence tools, Horizon identified both areas of success and potential gaps, enabling data-informed strategic modifications to tailor services for diverse patient needs, thereby enhancing inclusivity.[58]

Outcomes

- **Enhanced patient experience:** The institution of culturally aware healthcare practices resulted in a significant 25% improvement in patient satisfaction scores. Feedback

---

[55]. Amy C. Edmondson. *The Fearless Organization: Creating Psychological Safety in the Workplace for Learning, Innovation, and Growth.* Hoboken, NJ: Wiley, 2018.

[56]. Michael C. Hyter and Judith L. Turnock. *The Power of Inclusion: Unlock the Potential and Productivity of Your Workforce.* Hoboken, NJ: Wiley, 2020.

[57]. Mary-Frances Winters. *We Can't Talk about That at Work!: How to Talk about Race, Religion, Politics, and Other Polarizing Topics.* Oakland, CA: Berrett-Koehler Publishers, 2017.

[58]. Iris Bohnet. *What Works: Gender Equality by Design.* Cambridge: Belknap Press, 2016.

emphasized a higher appreciation for tailored care and acknowledgment of cultural diversities, highlighting Horizon's commitment to enhancing patient experiences by adapting practices to meet individual needs comprehensively.
- **Improved departmental synergy:** The nurturing of a collaborative approach among departments marked a substantial positive shift, leading to streamlined operations and more effective workflow management. This synergy fostered a work environment that valued diverse perspectives, ensuring inclusivity and empowerment across all departments.
- **Increased cultural competency:** Continuous educational opportunities bolstered the staff's cultural competency, leading to improved relationships with patients and colleagues alike. Team members became adept at navigating cultural nuances, thereby providing superior care and establishing a workplace culture that embraced inclusivity.

Insights

- **Proactive data application:** The pivotal role of data analytics in assessing initiative effectiveness and guiding DEI strategy enhancements was apparent. Real-time data facilitated proactive and informed decisions, demonstrating the necessity of such an approach for sustained DEI progress.
- **Continuous education empowerment:** The critical role of ongoing educational programs in maintaining DEI momentum was underscored. Horizon's continuous training initiatives reaffirmed the importance of equipping healthcare professionals with the tools to

implement DEI effectively, driving long-term cultural transformation.[59]

Through strategic foresight, leadership involvement, and technological and educational empowerment, Horizon Health Services has significantly improved its service to a diverse clientele while strengthening its internal culture.[60] This case exemplifies how a dedicated approach to DEI can lead to substantial organizational advancements, offering a model for other institutions aiming to enhance their own cultural frameworks.

Discussion questions

1. What challenges did Horizon Health Services face when trying to integrate DEI principles into its organizational framework? How did demographic shifts influence this need?

2. How did Horizon's strategic visioning contribute to the successful integration of DEI principles within the organization? What steps were crucial to creating an effective roadmap for DEI?

3. In what ways did leadership engagement platforms facilitate the discussion and application of DEI strategies at Horizon Health Services? How did these forums contribute to fostering a culture of continuous learning?

4. How did Horizon Health Services leverage technology and advanced analytics tools to track and enhance its

---

59. Kark Kaplan and Mason Donovan. *The Inclusion Dividend: Why Investing in Diversity & Inclusion Pays Off*. New York: Bibliomotion, 2013.

60. Dr. DeAnna Kimbrel-Hopkins, *Strategically Strengthen Your Leadership: Master DEI Challenges* (2025).

DEI progress? In what ways did data-driven decisions improve patient care and inclusion?

5. Discuss the impact of enhanced patient experiences and departmental synergy on Horizon Health Services' overall service delivery. How do these outcomes reflect the effectiveness of their DEI strategy?

6. How did Horizon's focus on continuous educational opportunities improve cultural competency among staff? What were the long-term benefits of enhanced cultural awareness in patient and colleague interactions?

7. What did Horizon Health Services learn about the role of data analytics in sustaining DEI initiatives? How can real-time data influence DEI strategies and their outcomes?

8. In what ways did ongoing education support Horizon in maintaining DEI momentum? How essential is continuous training in driving cultural transformation within healthcare environments?

9. How can other healthcare institutions apply the strategies and insights from Horizon Health Services to their own DEI initiatives? What are the potential barriers they might face, and how can they overcome them?

Chapter 5
Organizations' Role in Developing Leaders

Key Learning Objectives:
- Leadership development
- Organizational support for leaders
- Inclusive leadership and talent strategy
- Understanding communication styles
- Systemically leveraging cultural differences
- Purpose-driven leadership

In this chapter, we will dive deeper into the concept of organizational support. Organizational support is important to leadership as it ensures the development and education of inclusive leaders. When leaders feel supported they are more likely to have the efficacy to lead.

5.1 Leadership: Inherited or Developed?

Organizations play a critical role in developing and nurturing leaders when they are tasked with leading others. While some individuals may possess innate leadership qualities, many skills required for effective leadership can be cultivated and refined through training and development. A common debate is the notion of whether leaders are born or built. According to Figure 5.1, the debate is nature versus nurture, examining whether leadership qualities are natural, or whether they can be developed over time through experience and education.

Figure 5.1 The Great Man Theory

04 — Leaders are born and not made.

03 — Most of the leadership comes from the upper class of society.

02 — A small number of leaders come from the lower class of society.

01 — This theory contributed to the idea that leadership had something to do with inheritance and breeding.

Source: *The Decision Lab. "Great Man Theory."* https://thedecisionlab.com

A theory entitled, "Great Man Theory," states that leadership is a characteristic that people are born with, meaning that some people naturally possess certain traits like charisma, confidence, intelligence, and social skills. This theory also suggests that these skills can not be taught and can only be acquired at birth. Examples are those people who have natural abilities at a young age.[61]

Figure 5.2 explains transformational leadership, the counterargument to the Great Man Theory. This theory describes leaders as transformational and who can be taught the skills to be effective. According to this theory, leadership is a set of skills that can be taught and developed over time. The teachings of this theory argue that through proper education, training, and experience, individuals can develop effective leadership skills. This ideology promotes personal development, situational leadership, and self-awareness. Through this theory it is assumed that some characteristics can be inherited, however, most leadership traits can be learned over time.[62]

---

[61]. Benmira, Sihame, and Moyosolu Agboola. "Evolution of leadership theory." *BMJ leader* (2021): leader-2020.

[62]. Madi Odeh, Rana BS, Bader Yousef Obeidat, Mais Osama Jaradat, Ra'ed Masa'deh, and Muhammad Turki Alshurideh. "The transformational leadership role in achieving organizational resilience through adaptive cultures: the case of Dubai service sector." *International Journal of Productivity and Performance Management* 72, no. 2 (2023): 440-468.

Figure 5.2 Transformational Leadership Theory

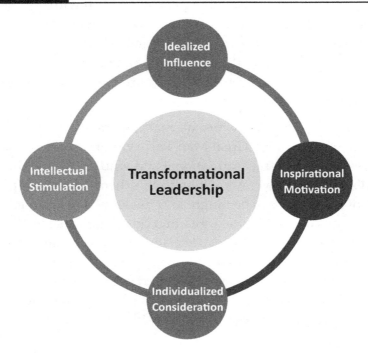

Source: *Transformational Leadership." Corporate Finance Institute,* https://corporatefinanceinstitute.com

Although these two perspectives are still debatable, it's safe to say they each play an important role in inclusive leadership. There are certain qualities that leaders must have to be effective; however, additional traits are needed to be truly inclusive.

Although leaders may have some innate traits, they should also continue to develop and grow their understanding and ability to cultivate and foster inclusive teams and environments. By investing time in learning and engaging in more cultural experiences, you will be more likely to authentically implement DEI practices.

5.1.1 Organizational support for leadership

Organizations have a particular responsibility to support leaders through the process of being more inclusive and effective. This investment can come in many forms such as training, tools, and resources to monitor and track effectiveness, as well as the power to make key decisions within an organization.

Organizations that invest in mentorship and sponsorship programs are able to develop more effective leaders. Developing relationships across the organization encourages connectedness and belonging. Additionally, through mentorship building, team members are able to share knowledge and gain more exposure to the different facets of the organization. Sponsorship promotes advocacy for teams that may have less visibility within the organization creating more access to opportunity. Through properly implementing and funding these programs, organizations demonstrate their commitment to DEI and inclusive leadership.

When organizations are intentional about providing opportunities for people of marginalized groups, their commitment to DEI becomes tangible and more than just statements. When team members feel the priority put on their overall well-being, they are likely to increase engagement and resilience. A strong and authentic commitment from the organization is also essential to the success of inclusive leaders.[63]

When organizations haven't traditionally focused on DEI, diversity tends to diminish in roles at the senior level. Therefore, it's important to recognize these trends

---

63. Eisenberger, Robert, Linda Rhoades Shanock, and Xueqi Wen. "Perceived organizational support: Why caring about employees counts." *Annual Review of Organizational Psychology and Organizational Behavior* 7 (2020): 101-124.

and implement programming and strategies to address the discrepancies. Programs that focus on developing and properly placing talent of diverse backgrounds are critical to growing the future of diversity within the organization and allowing it to evolve as society continues to change. A focus on these practices will also allow the organization to position and brand itself as a champion for DEI which will attract and retain more diverse talent.[64]

5.1.2 Implementing an inclusive talent strategy

As an inclusive leader, you want to ensure that you and others bring team members into the organization through inclusive practices. According to Figure 5.3, these strategies should focus on ensuring that opportunities are accessible to all, regardless of background, identity, or abilities. When team members are hired, there should be a sense of belonging and value. The inclusive voice of the organization should start at the attraction phase of the interview process. This starts with the intention reflected in the job postings and the language in the descriptions. Language should avoid alienating words based on gender, race, religion, and other demographics. Additionally, there should be a particular focus on unbiased evaluation and interviewing processes.

---

64. Huning, Tobias M., Kevin J. Hurt, and Rachel E. Frieder. "The effect of servant leadership, perceived organizational support, job satisfaction and job embeddedness on turnover intentions: An empirical investigation." In *Evidence-Based HRM: A Global Forum for Empirical Scholarship*, vol. 8, no. 2, pp. 177-194. Emerald Publishing Limited, 2020

Figure 5.3 Why does diversity hiring matter?

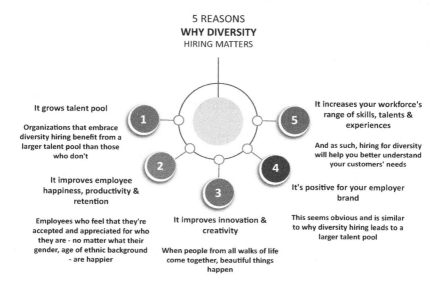

Source: Verlinden, *Neelie. n.d. "5 Reasons Why Diversity Hiring Matters (And How to Go about it)." Academy to Innovate HR. https://www.aihr.com*

However, recruitment is where the inclusive voice of the organization stops. The organization is responsible for implementing inclusivity at all levels not limited to but including the following:

- Flexible working arrangements for those with caregiving responsibilities
- Religious observances
- Robust anti-discrimination policies

It's important to remember that inclusive recruitment and retention are continuous processes that require full commitment from the organization. The goal should never be simply to just yield diverse talent, but to ensure all employees have the tools, resources, and space to be successful. This creates increased performance for the organization, the work they do, and their workforce.

5.2 Purpose Driven Leadership

5.2.1 Defining purposeful leadership

As an inclusive leader, having a clear purpose for the work you do will allow you to be intentional and authentic in creating inclusive and equitable spaces. It's also important to understand how your values of inclusion align with your organization's vision and values. When there is a lack of alignment, there is little to no space to implement change around inclusion and equity. It's important for many inclusive leaders to work within organizations whose values align with their own. This approach to leadership is often called purpose-driven leadership.

Purpose-driven leaders often hold the belief that an ethical purpose is at the forefront of the work they do, and are open to different perspectives from people of diverse backgrounds. When you have a commitment to a purpose beyond profits and a focus on social impact, you will be able to effectively demonstrate your commitment to inclusivity. This will help with breaking down barriers within an organization and fostering more collaboration. When leaders are able to perform their purpose, they are more likely to create environments that are highly inclusive, innovative, and cohesive.

Purpose is what sets the foundation for inclusive leadership and creates space for respect and understanding. When leaders can prioritize purpose, they cultivate a workplace that not only celebrates diversity but can leverage it for strategic advancement.

5.2.2 Cultivating purposeful leadership

Developing your purpose as an inclusive leader is an introspective process that requires a clear understanding and commitment to your values and goals. This includes the following steps:

- Take the time to reflect on your values and the roots of your beliefs.
- Determine the areas of your life where you are most strong and weak.
- Determine your leadership goals as they relate to your overall purpose.
- Get feedback from those who have experienced you as a leader to determine opportunities to grow.

With a focus on introspection, growth, and authenticity, you will craft a purpose that aligns with who you are professionally and personally.

5.2.3 The evolution of purposeful leadership

Historically, leadership focused on the monetary advancements of the organization. However, today, leaders are increasingly motivated by the people they serve and the impact of their work on individuals and communities.[65]

A leader with a clear purpose has a vision for work that goes beyond financial gains. Over the past several years,

---

65. Maheshwari, Anil K. "Workplace Well-being From Development of Consciousness Through Purposeful Leadership." *Journal of Management, Spirituality & Religion* 21, no. 2 (2024): 206-223.

many leaders have begun to focus more on the advancement of society and the environment. These leaders lead with an eye for authenticity, empathy, and ethics.

Many organizations have also taken on a purpose-driven approach that allows them to attach and retain diverse groups of customers and employees. Even though commitments to particular purposes can also cost organizations customers and employees, sticking to a clear purpose demonstrates authenticity for organizations, and will pay off in the long run.

5.2.4 Traits of purpose-driven leaders

As leaders become more and more focused on purpose-driven work, there are several traits to define a purpose-driven leader.[66] Purpose-driven leaders:

- Are focused more on values than profit
- Strive to be authentic and engage with team members empathically
- Are committed to cultivating work environments that are ethical, holding everyone to the same standards of ethical practices
- Ensure their overall purpose aligns with the organizations they attach themselves to
- Ensure they actively address social issues and use their voices to fight injustices
- Are committed to having a positive impact on those around them while reaching significant goals

---

66. van Knippenberg, Daan. "Meaning-based leadership." *Organizational Psychology Review* 10, no. 1 (2020): 6-28.

Chapter Summary

- Organizations play a critical role in developing and nurturing leaders when they are tasked with leading others. While some individuals may possess innate leadership qualities, many skills required for effective leadership can be cultivated and refined through training and development.

- Organizations have a particular responsibility to support leaders through the process of being more inclusive and effective. This investment can come in many forms, such as training, tools, and resources to monitor and track effectiveness, as well as the power to make key decisions within an organization.

- Organizations that invest in mentorship and sponsorship programs are able to develop more effective leaders. Developing relationships across the organization encourages connectedness and belonging.

- Programs that focus on developing and properly placing talent of diverse backgrounds are critical to growing the future of diversity within the organization and allowing it to evolve as society continues to change

- As an inclusive leader, you want to ensure that you and others bring team members into the organization through inclusive practices.

- It's important to remember that inclusive recruitment and retention are continuous processes requiring a full commitment from the organization. The goal should never be to just yield diverse talent but to ensure all employees have the tools, resources, and space to be successful.

- Developing your purpose as an inclusive leader is an introspective process that requires a clear understanding and commitment to your values and goals.

Quiz

1. **Organizations play a critical role in developing and nurturing leaders because:**
   a. Leadership skills happen overnight
   b. Leaders are required to develop their own skills
   c. Leadership is not an organization's issue
   d. None of the above

2. **The "Great Man Theory,":**
   a. Suggests that leadership is an inherent trait
   b. States that certain individuals naturally possess qualities such as charisma, confidence, intelligence, and social skills that make them effective leaders
   c. Suggests that these inherent traits are difficult, if not impossible, to teach, and those born with these qualities are predestined to lead
   d. All the above

3. **"Transformational Leadership Theory," is:**
   a. States that leadership skills can be taught and developed
   b. Argues that a leader can be created through proper training and experience
   c. There is a particular emphasis on the importance of personal development and situational awareness
   d. All the above

4. What are ways in which organizations can support leaders:
   a. There is no support to be offered
   b. Mentorship and sponsorship programs
   c. It is unethical to receive organizational support
   d. None of the above

5. Retention Strategies include:
   a. Flexible working arrangements for those with caregiving responsibilities
   b. Religious observances
   c. Robust anti-discrimination policies
   d. All the above

6. Purpose-driven leadership is important because:
   a. It plays an important role in fostering inclusive leadership
   b. Creates a hostile workplace environment
   c. Consider discrimination
   d. None of the above

7. Purpose-driven leadership is essential for inclusive leadership because:
   a. It sets a foundation for respect, empathy, and understanding across diverse groups
   b. It allows leaders to create an organizational culture that not only celebrates diversity but leverages it as a strategic advantage
   c. It not only benefits the individuals within the organization but also bleeds into society.
   d. All the above

8. Crafting a leadership purpose is an introspective journey that requires a deep understanding of one's:
   a. Values
   b. Strengths
   c. Aspirations
   d. All the above

9. Establishing clear leadership objectives that resonate with your values and mission will:
   a. Steer you towards your leadership purpose
   b. Question turmoil on your team
   c. Avoid clear communication
   d. None of the above

10. How do you create an effective leadership purpose:
    a. Consistent introspection
    b. Learning
    c. Evolution
    d. All the above

Answers

1 – d	2 – d	3 – d	4 – b	5 – d
6 – a	7 – d	8 – d	9 – a	10 – d

CHAPTER 6
Implementing Different Leadership Traits

Key Learning Objectives
- Authentic leadership
- Empathetic leadership
- Emotionally intelligent leadership
- The power of feedback and self-leadership
- Consequences of exclusionary leadership

Chapter six serves as an analysis of different leadership traits related to becoming an inclusive leader. This chapter will review key points to help you build competency and develop an inclusive leadership mindset. The goal of this chapter is to provide you with the definitions and strategies to create a leadership identity that is unique yet impactful around DEI.

6.1 Authentic and Empathetic Leadership

We explored different leadership styles in Chapter One. Authenticity is one of the key traits of an inclusive leader. Authentic leaders can be characterized as genuine and transparent, which is usually done naturally and effortlessly. They are true to themselves and their values, this can be seen in how they inspire others and build trust and loyalty through honesty and integrity.

What's great about authentic leaders is that they are not afraid to show vulnerability or admit mistakes. Also, strong relationships are built on mutual respect between friends, colleagues, and those they may manage. Authentic leaders are also aware of themselves and the world around them and can think outside of their surroundings. A keen understanding of their strengths and weaknesses allows them to lead with humility and empathy. By staying true to their beliefs and values, authentic leaders can create a positive and inclusive work environment where individuals feel empowered and motivated to achieve common goals.[67]

6.1.1 Fostering empathy as an authentic leader

As an inclusive leader understanding the power of empathy is invaluable. Empathy in leadership can be demonstrated through a focus on sharing the feelings of others. This means that you can connect with others and relate to their emotions and experiences as well as give compassion, and consider diverse perspectives. The key traits of an empathic and inclusive leader include active listening, genuine concern for people, and creating a supportive and

---

[67]. Saha, Surajit, Roshni Das, Weng Marc Lim, Satish Kumar, Ashish Malik, and Bharat Chillakuri. "Emotional intelligence and leadership: insights for leading by feeling in the future of work." *International Journal of Manpower* 44, no. 4 (2023): 671-701.

inclusive environment. Leaders should do the following to include empathy in their leadership style:[68]

- Leaders should be intentional about creating a safe space to talk. Safe spaces are physical and psychological spaces where team members can freely express their thoughts, ideas, and concerns. Consider implementing this into your leadership routine through regular team meetings, one-on-one sessions, or anonymous feedback channels.
- Leaders should also be role models. This is done through demonstrating empathy in their actions and interactions. This will allow you to set a powerful precedent for those around you. This looks like incorporating understanding, kindness, and compassion into daily leadership routines.
- Leaders should also be a source of support and resources. When leaders are empathic they not only listen but provide assistance and necessary resources. This support might help people overcome key challenges hindering growth. This can be demonstrated through offering training, mentoring, or guidance.
- Leaders are key to fostering a positive environment. They should be laser-focused on developing a positive and supportive work environment. This is most effectively done through implementing policies that promote work-life balance, recognize achievements, and prioritize mental health and well-being.
- Leaders should also develop a habit of continuous learning and empathy. The skills of empathy can be honed over time. There's no real beginning and ending

---

68. Einola, Katja, and Mats Alvesson. "The perils of authentic leadership theory." *Leadership* 17, no. 4 (2021): 483-490.

point but a commitment to continuous development. This continuous development can look like training, reading, and seeking feedback from others to enhance.

6.1.2 Fostering emotional intelligence as an authentic leader

Emotional intelligence is the ability to foster understanding, empathy, and collaboration within organizational teams on community structures. Emotional intelligence is significant to inclusive leadership as it allows you to understand and manage the emotions of yourself and others. This is a crucial trait for leaders to develop while growing an inclusive mindset. Inclusive leaders should create an environment where team members feel valued, respected, and included. When emotional intelligence is implemented properly and authentically, it can help better understand others' perspectives and emotions, improve communication, and build stronger relationships.[69]

When a leader acquires high emotional intelligence, they are more likely to recognize and manage their own emotions, as well as understand and respond to the emotions of others. With these unique skills, leaders are enabled to navigate complex social dynamics, resolve conflicts effectively, and promote inclusive cultures. By demonstrating empathy, listening actively, and showing genuine care for their team members, emotionally intelligent leaders can create a safe and supportive space where everyone's voice is heard and valued.

Additionally, when leaders develop a capacity for emotional intelligence it further supports inclusive

---

69. Nowack, Kenneth, and Paul Zak. "Empathy enhancing antidotes for interpersonally toxic leaders." *Consulting Psychology Journal: Practice and Research* 72, no. 2 (2020): 119.

leadership, since it empowers leaders to connect authentically, build trust, and cultivate a culture of belonging. When leaders have prioritized emotional intelligence and incorporated it into their overall leadership style, they are more likely to influence positive change, increase diversity, and inclusion, and enhance team performance and organizational success. The following are ways that leaders can develop a positive and inclusive work environment:[70]

- Leaders need to be self-aware. This starts with understanding emotions, strengths, weaknesses, and how you may be impacting others.
- Leaders need to be able to self-regulate. When a leader can control their emotions and impulses, they can react more effectively in difficult situations and conflicts.
- Leaders should continuously work on their social skills. This is important in developing strong relationships.
- Motivation is also a key factor that will allow leaders to be guided by their motivations rather than the agenda of others.

6.1.3 Fostering feedback as an authentic leader

As an inclusive leader, the power of giving and receiving feedback will be imperative to your success. Constructive feedback creates an environment of trust and open communication. When you provide feedback to your team members you demonstrate a value for diverse perspectives and the contributions of others, regardless of background. This is an example of how to increase inclusivity on

---

[70]. Rahman, Syahrir. "Emotional intelligence and leader effectiveness: A conceptual paper." *International Journal of Innovation and Business Strategy (IJIBS)* 15, no. 2 (2021).

your team that can help build a sense of belonging and psychological safety leading to increased engagement and productivity.

Feedback is also an essential part of personal and professional growth. In the spirit of inclusivity, feedback is not only about pointing out areas for improvement but also highlighting strengths and achievements. With a constructive feedback structure, people gain the ability to learn and develop their skills, ultimately contributing to overall success.

Feedback is also key in addressing biases and promoting diversity. As an inclusive leader, feedback should be used as a tool to recognize and challenge discriminatory behaviors or practices within an organization. Through seeking diverse perspectives and feedback, leaders can create a culture that embraces differences and values the unique contributions of people from diverse backgrounds.[71]

In practice, leaders should seek feedback from various sources to continue to develop. Engaging with trusted partners like peers, mentors, and team members to obtain diverse viewpoints will also help with the growth of inclusive mindsets. This feedback can be used to improve your methods and progress as a leader. It is also advantageous to consistently educate yourself on current leadership strategies and trends. Staying updated on various leadership approaches and methods, adapting them to suit your style and the dynamics of those you encounter, remaining authentic, seeking feedback, and staying informed will allow you to lead with authenticity and effectiveness. With a goal of continuous learning and self-improvement,

---

[71]. Lee, Yeunjae, and Jarim Kim. "Cultivating employee creativity through strategic internal communication: The role of leadership, symmetry, and feedback seeking behaviors." *Public relations review* 47, no. 1 (2021): 101998.

the journey of inclusive leadership is very much feasible. Below are some steps to further develop your leadership capabilities:

- Engage in relevant workshops and conferences that focus on networking with like-minded professionals with a focus on new insights and strategies.
- Find leadership books and articles that resonate with your leadership passion and purpose. This can help with self-motivation and staying abreast of best practices in leadership.
- Develop mentorship relationships. Finding the right mentor or mentee who can provide guidance and support can be essential on your leadership journey.
- Self-reflect on your interactions with others and develop strategies to engage according to inclusive practices. Through a consistent process of self-reflection, you will be able to recognize areas for growth and self-correct.
- Creating a positive culture that yields open feedback will help everyone grow within the organization.
- Developing an environment that promotes innovation and new ideas can help you adapt to changing circumstances and lead more effectively.

6.2 Self-Leadership, Awareness, and Bias

6.2.1 Self-leadership

Self-leadership is when a leader takes initiative, sets obtainable goals, and motivates themselves and others to achieve personal and professional success. This involves being proactive, disciplined, and self-aware to effectively navigate challenges and opportunities. Creating an inclusive environment is inevitable for leaders who practice self-leadership, take responsibility, and make decisions based on values and beliefs. When effectively implementing self-leadership skills, new opportunities are created for personal growth and career advancement. Here are some key strategies to enhance self-leadership:

- Setting clear and attainable goals is imperative for a self-guided leader. This can involve establishing both short-term and long-term objectives. This practice can increase focus and motivation.
- Effectively managing time is a key strategy for self-leadership. This includes developing procrastination avoidance strategies, meeting deadlines, and maintaining productivity. Technology can help here with virtual calendars and to-do lists to organize and track progress.
- Building resilience is a strategy that allows leaders to manage and overcome adversity.

6.2.2 Self-awareness

Self-awareness is an important trait to develop as you grow your inclusive mindset. The first step starts with fostering empathy and understanding. As you become more self-aware, you will be able to recognize your own biases. This becomes even more important for making fair and unbiased decisions. When you are able to develop a self-aware lens, leaders are better equipped to understand and appreciate the perspectives and experiences of others. This can create a more inclusive and diverse work environment. A high level of self-awareness can help you build trust and collaboration on your team. This can drive organizational success and help you reach your inclusion goals.

6.2.3 Debiasing through self-awareness

Your biases will become more apparent to you as you become more self-aware. It will also impact the way you perceive and interact with the world around you beyond the workplace. By becoming more aware of your own biases, you will be able to recognize the mindsets and prejudices that influence your outlook and decision-making. If you fail to acknowledge your own biases, you won't have the ability to truly develop as an inclusive leader. As you become more self-aware, you will readily identify your blind spots. Below are some practices to become more self-aware:

- Practice more mindfulness activities such as meditation or deep breathing.
- Writing down your thoughts and experiences can provide insights into interactions with others. You can use journaling as a tool for self-discovery and growth.
- Use leadership and personality tests to assess communication styles and characteristics to understand areas of development.
- Use feedback surveys from those that engage with you regularly.

6.3 Cultivating a Unique Inclusive Leadership Identity

Over the last several decades, various leadership styles have been coined. However, it is crucial for you to establish an inclusive leadership identity that is unique to you and your vision of leadership. This can be a difficult process, but it's critical to understand your uniqueness, values, beliefs, and strengths. Knowing who you are and who you want to be as a leader will allow you to genuinely cultivate inclusive environments. Your leadership identity will also allow you to embrace inclusivity by actively seeking diverse perspectives, listening to a variety of voices, and fostering a culture of inclusion.

Using your inclusive leadership strategy, you will be able to create a solid identity using the steps below:

- Create an inclusive leadership framework.
- Set commitments around diversity and inclusion that align with your values and culture.
- Drive diversity, equity, and inclusion initiatives.
- Be a role model of inclusive practices.
- Develop empathy as an approach to engaging with others.
- Hold yourself and others accountable for inclusivity.

6.3.1 Developing an Inclusive Mindset

Throughout this book, we've discussed developing an inclusive mindset frequently. This is a continuous process of learning and adopting inclusive leadership skills. As a leader, an inclusive mindset is one that constantly evolves to value and respect people of all different backgrounds.

Growing your inclusive mindset means challenging yourself to be willing to consider various viewpoints and experiences. It also means being an advocate for the injustices that come from a lack of inclusion and actively fighting for equity. This can be accomplished in the following ways:

- **Develop a sense of community:** Foster a team environment where people work toward common goals and values. This includes an environment where team members are comfortable sharing ideas and being creative.
- **Embrace differences:** Increase team engagement by embracing differences in culture, work styles, and communication styles in the workplace and other activities to help create a sense of ownership and representation.
- **Promote communication:** Understand the differences that exist on your team. This will allow you and your members to be more cohesive and have stronger bonds. This is done through communication and creating safe spaces for people to share who they are.

6.4 Consequences of Exclusionary Leadership

Leadership and DEI are often neglected when it comes to organizational priorities. However, when these structures can be properly implemented, they can have huge impacts on all facets of an organization. When there is a lack of inclusivity within a team or organization, it can lead to a work environment that can be toxic for employees and cause legal issues for the organization. Leaders are key to addressing and fixing these issues within the organization and creating spaces in which all employees feel seen and have access to opportunities. When leaders decide not to implement inclusive practices, they may:

- Alienate people of diverse backgrounds
- Decrease morale and productivity, and increase turnover rates
- Hinder safe spaces for creativity and innovation

There are also consequences when organizations decide not to uphold inclusive leadership practices, which include facing a negative reputation or lawsuits. Also, there can be scrutiny from customers, partners, and other stakeholders.

Chapter Summary

- As you continue your journey of becoming an inclusive leader, it's important to set realistic goals that measure your progress and success around inclusive people-centered practices.
- As an inclusive leader, the ability to attract and retain a diverse team is crucial to meeting organizational needs.
- It's important to be strategic about how you engage team members in order to attract, retain, and leverage the power of diverse experiences and perspectives. An effective strategy is to develop and implement a mentorship program.
- When team members of diverse backgrounds have extra support from those who have already been established within the organization, they are provided with the tools to break through barriers and increase access to opportunities.
- Investing in and implementing strategies to further engage diverse teams should include a clear and actionable roadmap.
- Your biases will become more apparent to you as you become more self-aware. It will also impact the way you perceive and interact with the world around you beyond the workplace.
- Where there is a lack of inclusivity on a team or throughout an organization, it can create a toxic work environment that can be toxic for employees and cause legal issues for the organization.

Quiz

1. What are the traits that contribute to authenticity in a leader?

    a. Not afraid to show vulnerability or admit mistakes
    b. Aware of themselves and the world around them
    c. A keen understanding of their strengths and weaknesses
    d. All the above

2. Jennifer is on a journey to becoming a more inclusive and empathetic leader. What is an important step she should take?

    a. She should work on being a role model for her team members
    b. She should ignore the needs of her team members to get work done
    c. She should assume everything is ok if no one says anything
    d. All the above

3. Emotional intelligence is significant to inclusive leadership because:

    a. It allows you to understand and manage the emotions of yourself and others
    b. It provides the ability to foster understanding, empathy, and collaboration
    c. It creates an environment where team members feel valued, respected, and included
    d. All the above

4. Chris is talking to this manager about increasing his emotional intelligence; however, he doesn't know where to start. As Chris' manager, what advice would you give him?
   a. Don't worry, it will happen naturally
   b. Emotions have no place at work
   c. Start by working on self-awareness. This starts with understanding emotions, strengths, weaknesses, and how you may be impacting others
   d. All the above

5. What are some ways to use feedback to increase inclusion within your teams?
   a. Constructive feedback creates an environment of trust and open communication
   b. Demonstrates a value for diverse perspectives and the contributions of others, regardless of background
   c. It's an essential part of personal and professional growth
   d. All the above

6. As a leader in your organization how do you give feedback about discriminatory behavior?
   a. Leave the feedback up to someone else
   b. Refuse to talk to others and the problem will go away
   c. Create a plan to listen to all parties involved and work with appropriate parties to resolve the issue
   d. All the above

7. Why is self-leadership important in becoming an inclusive leader?
   a. Self-leadership isn't a leadership strategy
   b. It helps leaders be more proactive, disciplined, and self-aware to effectively navigate challenges and opportunities
   c. Leaders don't need to be developed
   d. All the above

8. Paul is interested in a promotion to a leadership role. As his mentor, he asked you what steps he can take to be a better leader. How would you respond?
   a. Become more self-aware and learn your own biases
   b. Sit at the leader's table
   c. It will come naturally
   d. All the above

9. What are ways to become more self-aware?
   a. Practice more mindfulness activities such as meditation or deep breathing
   b. Write down your thoughts and experiences can provide insights into interactions with others. You can use journaling as a tool for self-discovery and growth
   c. Use leadership and personality tests to assess communication styles and characteristics to understand areas of development
   d. All the above

10. What is a leader's identity:
    a. Something used at jobs for management
    b. A style of leadership that is unique to you and fits your vision
    c. A task that society assigns to groups of people
    d. All the above

Answers

1 – d	2 – a	3 – d	4 – c	5 – d
6 – c	7 – b	8 – a	9 – d	10 – b

Chapter 7
Building Effective Teams as an Inclusive Leader

Key Learning Objectives
- Elements of an effective team
- A review of team dynamics
- Developing a common vision
- Communicating effectively across diverse teams
- Implementing cross-cultural communication skills

In this chapter, we explore the concepts of developing teams through inclusive leadership. Leaders who value inclusivity and forming effective teams play a crucial role in cultivating a positive work environment and reaching organizational goals. For leaders to truly be inclusive, they must establish a successful team that is built on diversity, equity, and inclusion principles. Embracing the distinct viewpoints, backgrounds, and experiences of each team member can lead to innovation and improved problem-solving skills. One of the main elements of effective inclusive leadership is to foster open communication and collaboration while ensuring that every voice is respected and acknowledged.

7.1 Elements of an Effective Team

Inclusive leaders should be paying particular attention to fostering a culture of trust and mutual respect among all team members. This is best demonstrated through showing transparency in your decision-making processes and creating an inclusive environment. In practice, this looks like promoting teamwork and offering opportunities for professional development.

As a leader, when you can put the success and welfare of your team at the forefront of all you do, you can build a cohesive and resilient team that flourishes and fosters respect.[72] Following these steps can lead to more effective teams:

- Create a culture of trust and mutual respect.
- Lead with transparency to establish an inclusive work environment.
- Encourage teamwork.
- Support professional growth for all team members.
- Prioritize well-being to promote unity and cooperation.
- Provide open communication channels within the team to build trust.
- Provide opportunities for continuous learning and development to support the professional growth of the team.

---

72. Roberson, Quinetta, and Jamie L. Perry. "Inclusive leadership in thought and action: A thematic analysis." *Group & Organization Management* 47, no. 4 (2022): 755-778.

7.1.1 A review of team dynamics

It's important to remember that when implementing inclusive leadership practices, you must understand the different types of teams you may come in contact with. Below are a few of the different team structures that may arise in the workplace:[73]

1. **Interdisciplinary teams:** Teams are based on the similarities of their work, like human resources, legal, marketing, etc.
2. **Cross-interdisciplinary teams:** Teams are composed of members from different job functions who come together to work on a project. These teams promote diverse perspectives, innovation, and creativity.
3. **Virtual teams:** Working remotely, virtual teams are now very common. These team members work in geographically different areas and collaborate using technology such as video conferencing and project management tools. In these kinds of distant teams, effective communication and trust are essential for success.
4. **Self-directed teams:** In these teams, members have the ability to make decisions. These teams are most effective in quick decision-making and flexibility. Accountability is key here to achieve common goals.

7.1.2 Establishing a common vision

Establishing a clear purpose for the team can be a challenge for inclusive leaders. As discussed earlier in the book, it's important for leaders to develop a purpose for

---

[73]. Paulus, Paul B. "Fostering creativity in groups and teams." In *Handbook of organizational creativity*, pp. 165-188. Psychology Press, 2024.

themselves and their teams. This will help team members better understand their direction, goals, and the "why" behind the work they do. When a clear purpose has been defined, an environment that fosters a sense of unity, collaboration, and community can develop.[74]

First, leaders need to ensure everyone has a clear understanding of goals, values, and the role of the organization. When these objectives are aligned, there is a clear vision established which can lead to an increase in motivation and engagement. As a leader, you can also use the team vision to make effective decisions, prioritization, and allocation of resources. Team members are also able to understand where they stand within the organization and measure their level of success. A strong team purpose can also lead to a solid groundwork for teamwork, productivity, and helping to achieve goals.

A culture of inclusion means that leaders are committed to motivating all team members to utilize their unique skills and talents. Open dialogue can enhance everyone's understanding of the team's goals. When all team members are engaged in shaping the team's vision, it fosters a sense of ownership and commitment, which can significantly enhance productivity.

7.2 Sourcing and Selecting the Right Team Members

Finding the right team members is key to building a successful and diverse team where everyone feels included. The first step a leader must take to achieve this is to start with clearly defining the roles and responsibilities of the

---

74. Watkins, Michael D. "THE DISCIPLINE OF VISIONING FOR LEADERS." *Leader to Leader* 2024, no. 113 (2024): 87-91.

team. This will help to identify the specific skill sets and qualities required in potential team members.

Inclusive job posts are also another way leaders can be effective in attracting diverse talent. Reviewing job descriptions for equitable and inclusive language is an effective strategy to bring in more diverse talent. This can be achieved by looking for inclusive wording that encourages candidates from diverse backgrounds to apply. Another tactic would be to avoid using biased language or unnecessary gendered terms that could deter certain groups from applying. For example, using terms that are geared toward certain populations or groups of people.

Biased language in job descriptions perpetuates discrimination and limits opportunities to increase diversity in the workplace as some groups may not feel welcomed. For example, biased language can be seen in gender-specific terms like "salesmen" or "waitresses," which can discourage individuals of other genders from applying. Age-related biases may also be present, such as using language like "recent graduates" or "young and energetic" candidates, which can exclude older candidates. Also, using terms like "stronger" or "aggressive" to describe potential candidates may unintentionally convey biases to certain groups of people. It's important for leaders to review job descriptions for biased language and intentionally focus on inclusivity to attract a diverse and qualified applicant pool.

Additionally, assessing the qualifications and requirements to ensure they are truly necessary for the role will be key to success. Leaders should also consider if any job requirements could be barriers to underrepresented groups and if so, implement ways to decrease or eliminate those barriers. Leaders should also ensure that the job descriptions mention a commitment to diversity, equity, and inclusion within the organization.

7.2.1 Debiasing the hiring process

The act of debiasing qualifications on job descriptions will be an important step as an inclusive leader. This can be done by focusing on the actual skills and experiences required to do the job rather than on things that are more prevalent in certain groups like specific degrees or certifications. One way to address this is to consider specifying the skills and experience that are gained through that degree instead of listing a degree as a requirement.[75]

Using gender-neutral language in job descriptions to attract a diverse pool of applicants is also another strategy. Avoiding using masculine or feminine pronouns and terms that may unconsciously deter certain groups will also be very effective. Technology can also be an effective tool. Software like Textio or Gender Decoder can be used to analyze your job descriptions for biased language and suggest alternatives.

In the interviewing process bias can decrease by implementing a diverse panel of employees in the development and review of job descriptions. The different perspectives can provide important insights into how certain languages may lack inclusion of underserved groups.

Looking at the responsibilities outlined in the job description is another way to ensure language is inclusive. Doing these entails ensuring the responsibilities are equitable and do not burden some groups more than others. For example, when a job description is heavy on clerical work,

---

[75]. Nandigama, Dhanisha, and Aarti Shyamsunder. "Eeny, Meeny, Miny, Moe: Hire Him and Let Her Go? Using Science to Reduce Hiring Bias." *NHRD Network Journal* 14, no. 2 (April 2021): 259–73. https://doi.org/10.1177/2631454120987343.

it may give the impression that it is more geared toward women. Intentionality about the language in job descriptions through an equity and inclusion lens can help attract a diverse pool of candidates.

7.2.2 Sourcing diverse and qualified candidates

As an inclusive leader, you not only want to find the proper candidates but also attract them. The following are strategies to attract a diverse pool of candidates:

1. **Create relationships with diversity organizations:** Partnering with local diversity organizations, such as cultural associations, LGBTQ+ groups, or women in leadership networks helps to tap into networks and reach a more diverse candidate pool.
2. **Hold virtual career fairs:** This will allow you to reach candidates from different areas and backgrounds. Social media can promote virtual events and attract a wide range of potential candidates.
3. **Incorporate blind hiring strategies:** Using blind recruitment practices, such as removing names and personal information from resumes can help mitigate unconscious biases and put more focus on candidates' experiences and backgrounds.
4. **Implement referral programs:** Develop an incentive program to promote diversity by encouraging employees to refer candidates of different backgrounds for incentives.

7.2.3 Assessing diverse skills and qualifications

Leaders must also be intentional about the process of evaluating diverse candidates. This may require a different approach other than traditional metrics and processes. When assessing candidates from diverse backgrounds, transitional skills like cultural awareness, adaptability, effective communication skills, and keen emotional intelligence can be very valuable.[76]

Cultural awareness in candidates of diverse backgrounds is essential for the overall understanding and integration of different cultural norms and perspectives into the workplace. When organizations can be flexible in the skills and qualifications they seek, they can evaluate a candidate's ability to thrive through a different lens. Attributes like the ability to adapt to changing circumstances and work effectively with individuals from various backgrounds can be key characteristics of candidates from diverse backgrounds. Strong communication skills are key in fostering collaboration and understanding among team members with diverse experiences. Emotional intelligence helps in managing relationships and resolving conflicts in a multicultural setting.

By assessing candidates based on these transitional skills and qualifications, employers can build a more inclusive workplace that values diversity and promotes mutual respect among all team members.

---

[76]. Tai, J., Ajjawi, R., Bearman, M., Boud, D., Dawson, P., & Jorre de St Jorre, T. (2023). Assessment for inclusion: Rethinking contemporary strategies in assessment design. *Higher Education Research & Development, 42*(2), 483-497.

7.3 Establishing Team Norms

Being an inclusive leader means you understand team norms required to create diverse and effective teams. For teams to normalize, they typically go through several phases before establishing clear working dynamics.[77] The first phase of team development is the formation of the team. This happens when team members are put together and get to know each other. This is also the phase where they understand each other's roles and responsibilities. In this phase, team norms may not be explicitly defined but are informally established through interactions and observations.

7.3.1 Managing conflicts in teams

As the team progresses, the storming phase may arise, where conflicts and differences in opinions surface. This stage is crucial for defining team norms as members work through disagreements and establish guidelines for communication and decision-making. This process helps the team clarify expectations and boundaries, leading to a more cohesive and productive group dynamic. Some examples of how to do this include:

- **Engage with active listening:** Participate fully in discussions by posing clarifying questions and summarizing key points to align team understanding. A phrase to use could be, "To ensure clarity, are you proposing...?"
- **Facilitate conflict resolution:** Address conflicts by emphasizing common objectives and transforming negative dynamics into productive dialogue. For

---

[77]. Levi, Daniel, and David A. Askay. *Group Dynamics for Teams*. 6th edition. Los Angeles London New Delhi Singapore Washington DC Melbourne: SAGE, 2021.

example, "Let's refocus on our shared goals and explore how different perspectives can contribute."
- **Clarify roles and responsibilities:** Clearly define and communicate roles to prevent confusion and overlap. Maintain an accessible document that outlines each team member's duties.
- **Establish boundaries and standards:** Hold a session to define appropriate behaviors and highlight standards necessary to uphold a constructive team environment.

7.3.2 Managing shared understanding among teams

The final stage in the team development process is in the norming phase. This is when the team solidifies its norms and values. This can create a shared understanding of how they will work together. There should be norms created around accountability, respect, collaboration, and feedback. These things are often formalized during the final stage to ensure continued success and effectiveness. However, once norms have been established, a regular review of these norms may be necessary as the team evolves over time.

Each team should go through the process of developing team norms. These steps are key for fostering an inclusive work environment where everyone feels a sense of belonging and has opportunities to thrive. When a team properly develops norms, these norms will act as a set of guidelines or expectations that team members should agree to follow in order to foster a sense of cohesiveness. In this process, it's important to involve all team members to ensure everyone's voice is heard.

The process of developing team norms starts with identifying the values and behaviors that are important to each member of your team. This can be things such as attitudes, communication styles, meeting etiquette, decision-making processes, and conflict resolution. As a leader, you should encourage open and honest communication among team members to establish a shared understanding of the norms.

Properly implementing the steps to develop team norms creates a supportive and respectful culture that can also motivate an increase in performance and teamwork. Effective team norms can enhance team cohesion, boost morale, and ultimately lead to better outcomes for the team as a whole.

7.4 Communicating Effectively Across Diverse Teams

As an inclusive leader, it's important to be able to effectively communicate vision and purpose. This starts with the ability to develop open and honest communication within the team. Inclusive leaders are responsible for creating a safe space for open discussions. When team members feel valued, they are more likely to engage with your vision. It's also the leader's responsibility to provide the team with clarity. The leader should ensure the vision is clear, concise, and easy to understand. Team members should also be able to communicate the leader's vision. To make sure the message is clear, the vision should be communicated through verbal and written channels using simple language and avoiding jargon to ensure everyone on your team can grasp the direction you want to take.

It is also important that leaders tailor their communication style to meet the needs of people from many backgrounds. Using different modes of communication like one-on-one meetings, group discussions, or virtual communication will work to make sure everyone feels included and heard. Nonverbal communication also plays a big role as the appropriate cues should be used to properly deliver messages.

7.4.1 Understanding cross-cultural communication

When a leader is able to understand that there are different styles of communication among different cultures, they can start to step into their inclusive leadership journey. Cultural communication styles can influence the way people send and understand messages. For example, in high-context cultures like in Asia, the Middle East, and South America, nonverbal cues, implicit meanings, and relationships dominate communication. In these cultures, people are more likely to read between the lines and prioritize peace. In low-context cultures like North America, Northern Europe, and Australia prefer direct communication, explicit language, and individualism. These cultures value clarity and efficiency in communication processes.[78]

Some cultures are also more hierarchical in the way they communicate. These cultures also place high priority on respect for authority and formal language. Whereas egalitarian cultures prioritize equality and open dialogue, promoting a more casual and participative communication approach. As an inclusive leader, understanding and respecting these different communication styles is essential for effective cross-cultural interactions and can help avoid misunderstandings or conflicts that may arise due to differing communication styles. When a leader is aware of diverse communication styles, they can adapt their own

---

78. Aririguzoh, Stella. "Communication competencies, culture and SDGs: effective processes to cross-cultural communication." *Humanities and Social Sciences Communications* 9, no. 1 (2022): 1-11.

style of communication to better connect with others from different cultural backgrounds.

Another important element is passion. Show your enthusiasm and belief in the vision you are sharing. Your team will be more likely to get on board if they see your genuine commitment and excitement about the future you are aiming to create together.

7.4.2 Implementing cross-cultural communication skills

As leaders become more aware of different communication styles, they must also become aware of how to implement different strategies to address those communication styles. The following are ways leaders can respond to cultural communication differences:

- **Participation in cultural sensitivity training:** Engage in workshops or courses that can provide valuable insights into different cultural norms, values, and communication styles. This will also help leaders develop a deeper understanding of how nonverbal cues are perceived in various cultures.
- **Active listening:** It is crucial, along with observing nonverbal cues. When a leader can listen attentively and show genuine interest in other's perspectives, they will be able to build trust and relationships across cultural boundaries.
- **Adaptability and flexibility:** Adjusting your communication styles is important when leading diverse teams. This includes modifying your own nonverbal communication to align with the cultural differences of team members.

- **Accepting constructive feedback:** Be open to feedback from team members from different cultures on your communication can provide valuable information to continue to grow as an inclusive leader.

Overall, as you develop into a more inclusive leader, it is most important to hear the voice of your team. Your team is integral to building and implementing a successful vision. Create a space where team members feel comfortable adding their input and being active participants in the process. When people feel heard and valued, they are more likely to be engaged and dedicated to achieving the shared vision.

Chapter Summary

- Leaders who value inclusivity and forming effective teams play a crucial role in cultivating a positive work environment and reaching organizational goals.
- Open communication shows transparency in the decision-making processes and creates an inclusive environment.
- Leaders need to ensure everyone has a clear understanding of goals, values, and the role of the organization.
- A culture of inclusion means that leaders are committed to motivating all team members to utilize their unique skills and talents.
- The first step a leader must take to achieve inclusion and equity is to start by clearly defining the roles and responsibilities of the team. This will help to identify the specific skill sets and qualities required in potential team members.
- Reviewing job descriptions for equitable and inclusive language is an effective strategy to bring in more diverse talent.
- Biased language in job descriptions perpetuates discrimination and limits opportunities to increase diversity in the workplace as some groups may not feel welcomed.
- Using gender-neutral language in job descriptions to attract a diverse pool of applicants is also another strategy.
- As the team progresses, the storming phase may arise, where conflicts and differences in opinions surface.
- A leader must be able to understand that there are different styles of communication among team members in order to actually have effective communication.

Quiz

1. As an inclusive leader building effective teams, it is important to understand different types of teams because:
   a. This will help you understand how to effectively form and lead the team
   b. All teams are the same
   c. Teams create their own dynamics
   d. All the above

2. Team structures can include:
   a. Interdisciplinary Teams
   b. Cross-interdisciplinary Teams
   c. Virtual Teams
   d. All the above

3. Self-Directed Teams are:
   a. Ineffective teams
   b. Used to make decisions
   c. Teams that have no leader
   d. All the above

4. Why is it important that leaders establish a common vision?
   a. There doesn't need to be a common vision
   b. Help team members better understand their direction, goals, and the 'why' behind the work they do
   c. This should only be done by senior leaders
   d. All the above

5. Kim is a new leader who aims to build an effective and diverse team. As her advisor, she asks you what the first step is. Your response is:
   a. Let the HR do it
   b. Pick people that act like and think like you
   c. Clearly define the roles and responsibilities of the team
   d. All the above

6. What are ways to attract diverse talent?
   a. Inclusive job posts
   b. Remove biased language in job descriptions.
   c. Assess the qualifications and requirements of the role to ensure they are truly necessary for the role.
   d. All the above

7. What are ways to de-bias qualifications on job descriptions?
   a. By focusing on the actual skills and experiences required to do the job rather than on things that are more prevalent in certain groups like specific degrees or certifications
   b. By focusing only on what is important to you
   c. By creating a dream candidate
   d. All the above

8. Lisa has an administrative support role open. However, she is consistently receiving applications from female candidates only. What are some ways to make her job postings more gender-neutral?
   a. Avoid using masculine or feminine pronouns and terms that may unconsciously deter certain groups.
   b. Software like Textio or Gender Decoder can be used to analyze your job descriptions for biased language and suggest alternatives.
   c. Host a focus group of people from different backgrounds to review and provide feedback on your job descriptions.
   d. All the above

9. How can you decrease bias in the interview process?
   a. This will happen naturally
   b. By implementing a diverse panel of employees in the development and review of job descriptions
   c. There's usually no bias in this process
   d. All the above

10. What are the best ways to source or find diverse talent?
    a. Create Relationships with Diversity Organizations
    b. Hold Virtual Career Fairs
    c. Incorporate Blind Hiring Strategies
    d. All the above

Answers

1 – a	2 – d	3 – b	4 – b	5 – c
6 – d	7 – a	8 – d	9 – b	10 – d

CHAPTER 8
Using Influence and Measuring Performance

Key Learning Objectives
- Understanding performance levels
- Using influence as a tool to increase performance
- Goal setting as a means to influence
- Setting SMART goals
- Professional development as a tool to increase equity

Chapter Eight provides an overview of how influence can be utilized as a tool for inclusive leadership. We provide knowledge about using influence to increase the performance levels of diverse teams. Additionally, the use of goals and professional development is explored as tools to increase inclusion and equity.

8.1 Assessing Performance

In your journey as an inclusive leader, understanding the importance of properly influencing performance outcomes is imperative. When determining how to assess performance, outcomes can be categorized into organizational, team, and individual.

As an Inclusive leader, measuring the performance of the organization can help determine the effectiveness of your efforts. When assessing the organizational outcomes you should be focused on overall success. Measures such as profitability, market share, customer satisfaction, and overall business growth must be considered. Outcomes should be measured over extensive periods and reflect the overall efforts of all functions within the organization.[79]

When considering the performance of a team, outcomes should be at the effectiveness of a group working towards a common goal. These measures should include team productivity, collaboration, communication, and the ability to meet deadlines and deliverables. As an inclusive leader, understanding how teams are performing to identify if teams are functioning cohesively and achieving objectives efficiently.

Additionally, determining how your efforts impact individuals in the organization is key. This can start with assessing performance outcomes for individuals focused on the success of each employee, which can be measured in a few different ways, such as individual productivity, quality of work, adherence to deadlines, skills development, and overall job satisfaction. The voices of employees are

---

[79]. Khan, H., Rehmat, M., Butt, T. H., Farooqi, S., & Asim, J. (2020). Impact of transformational leadership on work performance, burnout and social loafing: a mediation model. *Future Business Journal, 6*(1), 40.

so important as they will provide valuable feedback for improvement and knowledge to properly recognize their contribution.

8.2 Using Influence as a Tool to Increase Performance

Once you've become aware of how to assess success as an inclusive leader, you must understand how to influence high-level performance and outcomes. To effectively grow performance and outcomes within an organization, across teams and individually, it's important to have clear goals that are actionable and provide a sense of direction.

Maintaining a positive mindset will be essential on your journey as an inclusive leader. It will also be important to remain focused on the goals you set forth for the organization and yourself. This can be best achieved by continuously learning and developing skills to address issues, especially cultural issues that may arise in the workplace.

Having collaboration and effective communication with peers and team members will also enhance the performance of your team by tapping into collective strengths and fostering support. It's also very important to maintain a healthy work-life balance that considers the wellness of your staff and self.

8.3 Goal Setting: A Powerful Tool for Influence

As you continue your journey to becoming an inclusive leader, it's important to set realistic goals that measure your progress and success around inclusive people-centered practices. When setting goals, it's important to make sure your goals are aligned with the SMART model: Specific, Measurable, Achievable, Relevant, and Timely. Setting clear goals and objectives regarding the goals is very important for your team. Your team members should have a clear understanding of their roles and responsibilities.[80]

One of the first things to do would be to establish key performance indicators or KPIs. These indicators are important to help you track your goals. When developing your KPIs you should ensure they align with the overall vision, values, and objectives of the team and organization. Once you've determined your KPIs, they should be reviewed and evaluated regularly for contingencies and effectiveness. Setting and reaching goals can also be used to boost the morale of the team. This will allow the team to build cohesion over shared goals and vision.

8.3.1 Setting SMART goals and measuring success

As an inclusive leader, setting SMART goals is a powerful tactic to use to help you meet your people-centered goals. Some examples of SMART goals include:

1. **Specific:** "Increase a sense of belonging by 20% by the end of the quarter by launching a new cultural awareness campaign bringing awareness to the different demographics within the organization."

2. **Measurable:** "Reduce employee complaints by 50% within the next six months by implementing a new alternative resolution process."

---

80. Latham, Gary P. "Motivate employee performance through goal setting." *Principles of Organizational Behavior: The Handbook of Evidence-Based Management 3rd Edition* (2023): 83-111.

3. **Achievable:** "Complete an inclusive leadership course within the next year to increase leadership skills and develop an actionable toolbox."
4. **Relevant:** "Improve employee engagement scores by 15% over the next year by implementing a new development program to create a new pipeline to leadership."
5. **Timely:** "Update all job descriptions to ensure roles and language are inclusive by the end of the year."

As an inclusive leader, your SMART goals will help you create a roadmap for your work and will ensure it is clear, measurable, and attainable, leading to increased motivation, focus, and productivity. When evaluating your people-centered work around inclusion, a few areas you may focus on are metrics such as employee turnover rate, training, engagement, complaints, promotions, development participation, employee satisfaction, and attraction.

8.4 Retaining Diverse Populations

Studies have shown that the first step to increasing diversity within organizations starts before potential candidates even apply. This is considered the attraction phase. As an inclusive leader, the ability to attract and retain a diverse team is crucial to meeting organizational needs.

As we've discussed throughout this book, increasing diversity in candidate pools means ensuring the organization and your team are welcoming to people of different backgrounds. This not only includes language that states the organization is inclusive but also has tangible evidence of inclusivity. This is typically proven by employee testimonials. Additionally, it is important to show authentic interest in diverse populations by building relationships and engaging with different cultural associations and organizations.

Your role as an inclusive leader not only means attracting diverse talent but also retaining them. This can be done by providing intentional efforts toward professional development, mentorship programs, and creating an inclusive and equitable culture. You can also be effective in retaining diverse talent by offering additional benefits such as competitive compensation and benefits, flexible work schedules, and promotion opportunities.

8.4.1 Mentorship as a strategy for engaging diverse talent

It's important to be strategic about how you engage team members in order to attract, retain, and leverage the power of diverse experiences and perspectives. An effective strategy is to develop and implement a mentorship program. This will allow team members to access guidance and support from those who may have more experience or different skill sets. Developing affinity groups or employee resource groups can also be an effective strategy to engage team members. These groups often help employees foster a sense of community through engagement and bringing awareness to diverse backgrounds or identities.[81]

Activities in these groups may include networking, career development resources, supporting different aspects of the business, and serving as a platform for employees' personal and professional experiences and challenges.

---

81. Siegle, Del, D. Betsy McCoach, and Cindy M. Gilson. "Extending learning through mentorships." In *Methods and materials for teaching the gifted*, pp. 551-587. Routledge, 2021.

8.4.2 Sponsorship as a strategy to promote diverse teams

Another way to engage a team of diverse professionals is through implementing sponsorship programs. Sponsorship programs are different from mentorship programs as they focus on advocating for the advancement of people from marginalized backgrounds.

Sponsors are prominent people within the organization who can use their influence and networks to create opportunities. This might be done by recommending them for important projects, stretch assignments, promotion opportunities, or increasing their visibility.

When team members of diverse backgrounds have that extra support from those that have already been established within the organization they are provided with the tools to break through barriers and increase access to opportunities.

8.5 Professional Development: A Tool to Increase Equity

Investing in the development of your team is also an effective way to create an environment where everyone has the opportunity to thrive. However, this is an international practice that requires the leader to be an advocate for the tools and resources required to offer development opportunities to team members.

On your inclusive leadership journey, it's important to consider your own professional development. This is important because it will give you the tools to stay up-to-date with best practices, laws, and policies. As you continue to expand your knowledge around people, culture, and DEI you will be able to make more informed decisions and lead your team more efficiently.

Additionally, as an inclusive leader, when you act as a role model and show your commitment to growth and development, team members will also strive for that same level of excellence. The ability to inspire others is also an important trait in an inclusive leader, as it will allow for a more inclusive work environment.

8.5.1 Development plans: A strategic roadmap for diverse talent

Inclusive leadership is about having a vision of a work environment where people of all different backgrounds thrive. Investing in and implementing strategies to further engage diverse teams should include a clear and actionable roadmap. Most often these plans are called development plans. Development plans can help drive the growth and success of team members.

To properly develop and implement a strategic development plan, you can start by assessing the different skill levels within the team. This will allow you to gauge strengths and areas that need to be improved. After the assessment, you will then be able to set individual goals for each team member. Here, you can also implement the SMART goals model we discussed in the previous section. The most important part of this process is to ensure you have heard the voices of everyone on your team.

Once the goals have been set, determine the tools and resources needed to meet these goals. Prioritizing goals based on the resources that are more readily available will help to ensure the feasibility of the goals.

Lastly, it's important to have regular check-ins to understand progress and implement any contingencies that can help to keep the team member on track. Creating and intentionally working through development plans with your team will cultivate growth mindsets and a sense of belonging.

8.5.2 Feedback as a tool to increase equity

Another important tool to have in your inclusive leader toolbox is the art of giving effective feedback. Feedback is important for the personal and professional growth of your team members.[82] Here are some valuable ways to give constructive feedback to your team members:

1. **Be specific:** The best feedback is feedback that is specific. Make sure your comments are precise and include detailed examples of behaviors with clear options for improvement.
2. **Don't make it personal:** Keep feedback completely impersonal. Focus on tasks and outcomes rather than the personal attributes of the team member. This will remove bias and defensiveness.
3. **Include corrective action:** Ensure that feedback includes clear corrective actions. Consider how things can be done more effectively moving forward and any tools or resources that can be helpful.
4. **Use the sandwich approach:** Consider using the sandwich approach which will allow you to start by discussing strengths, then areas of improvement, and concluding

---

[82]. Sauder, Molly Hayes, and Jaime R. DeLuca. "The power of engaged reflection in fostering new insights on diversity, equity and inclusion." *Journal of Hospitality, Leisure, Sport & Tourism Education* 35 (2024): 100520.

with strengths again. This can help with having a more balanced conversation.

5. **Provide timely feedback:** Give feedback right away. Most often, feedback is given to team members once a year. However, it's too late to make corrections at that point. Therefore, it's important to give feedback as often as possible to allow room for growth and development. Consider providing feedback monthly or quarterly.

Chapter Summary

- As an inclusive leader, understanding how teams are performing is important to identify if teams are functioning cohesively and achieving objectives efficiently.
- As you continue your journey of becoming an inclusive leader, it's important to set realistic goals that measure your progress and success around inclusive people-centered practices.
- As an inclusive leader, the ability to attract and retain a diverse team is crucial to meeting organizational needs.
- It's important to be strategic about how you engage team members in order to attract, retain, and leverage the power of diverse experiences and perspectives. An effective strategy is to develop and implement a mentorship program.
- When team members of diverse backgrounds have extra support from those who have already been established within the organization, they are provided with the tools to break through barriers and increase access to opportunities.
- Investing in and implementing strategies to further engage diverse teams should include a clear and actionable roadmap.

Quiz

1. What are the best ways to assess performance within an organization?
   a. Organizational
   b. Team
   c. Individual
   d. All the above

2. Tom wants to measure the overall success of inclusion within the organization. As a strategist within the organization, what areas of analysis would you suggest?
   a. Measure profitability, market share, customer satisfaction, and overall business growth
   b. Measure changes in products
   c. This cannot be measured
   d. All the above

3. Tom also wants to measure the success of inclusion within this team. What would be the most appropriate measures?
   a. Measure customer satisfaction
   b. Team productivity, collaboration, communication, and the ability to meet deadlines and deliverables
   c. This cannot be measured
   d. All the above

4. Tom also wants to measure his own efforts as an inclusive leader. What measures should he focus on?
   a. Ask his team members for feedback
   b. Review the level of engagement
   c. Review the quality of work
   d. All the above

5. Why is maintaining a positive mindset essential for an inclusive leader?
   a. To have the ability to address cultural issues
   b. To have the ability to collaborate with peers and team members
   c. To have the ability to maintain a healthy work/life balance
   d. All the above

6. Establishing KPIs is important because:
   a. They are used to keep track of people
   b. They are focused on the customers
   c. They are aligned with the overall vision, values, and objectives of the team and organization
   d. All the above

7. "Increase a sense of belonging by 20% by the end of the quarter by launching a new cultural awareness campaign bringing awareness to the different demographics within the organization" is an example of what kind of goal?
   a. SMART goal
   b. Perfect goal
   c. People goal
   d. All the above

8. SMART goals are important because:
   a. They aren't a real thing
   b. They will help you create a roadmap for your work
   c. They won't help to ensure success
   d. All the above

9. What is the attraction phase in the hiring process?
   a. The step before people decide to apply for a job
   b. When you call someone for an interview
   c. The first day of work
   d. All the above

10. What is a key approach to creating a welcoming environment where people of diverse backgrounds feel comfortable joining?
    a. Create tangible evidence of inclusivity
    b. Prove inclusion with employee testimonials
    c. Show opportunities for people of diverse backgrounds
    d. All the above

Answers

1 – d	2 – a	3 – b	4 – d	5 – d
6 – c	7 – a	8 – b	9 – a	10 – d

CHAPTER 9
Developing and Implementing a Sustainable DEI Leadership Plan

Key Learning Objectives
- Developing and implementing a framework
- Gaining buy-in and investment from senior leadership
- Developing a communication plan
- Implementing a roll-out strategy
- Measuring outcomes, ROIs, and re-strategizing

Chapter Nine provides an overview of how to develop and implement a DEI plan. This chapter will discuss creating a framework, vetting the plan, and measuring success. Additionally, this chapter offers leaders with actionable steps to implement what was learned in the book.

9.1 Developing and Implementing a DEI Framework

As an inclusive leader, it's important that you have the skills to build a DEI framework for your team and stakeholders. This framework will assist you with creating an understanding of how DEI relates to the work you do and the people you lead and serve. This framework should include key strategies to promote an inclusive working environment where everyone can thrive. Some of the main areas this framework should focus on are the organization's commitment to DEI, assessments to understand organizational strengths and weaknesses, a strategic plan, action steps, and measures.[83]

9.1.1 Developing a DEI in leadership framework

As you build your framework, you want to make sure the organizational commitment to DEI is clear. This is one of the most important steps in the process as it requires you to engage with the senior leaders within your organization to ensure alignment around how DEI will be defined and carried out within an organization. Once alignment is established, there must be a clear commitment made. This commitment is usually reflected in organizational values and goals. However, as an inclusive leader, your goal should be to ensure that these values are not only stated but also lived. This can require different levels of accountability to see the changes you want to see as an inclusive leader. Some have adjusted organizational structures and budgets in order to hire a Chief Diversity Officer, additional tools and resources

---

83. White, Carla Y., Ami Patel, and Dominique Cossari. "Organizational commitment to diversity, equity, and inclusion: a strategic path forward." *American Journal of Health-System Pharmacy* 79, no. 5 (2022): 351-358.

for diverse populations, and established cultural awareness groups or employee resource groups.

Once you've gained the green light from your leadership team, it's important to assess the strengths and weaknesses of the organization. Here you will analyze (1) what the organization is doing around DEI and (2) how well they are doing it. Some key data points may include workforce demographics, climate surveys to understand employees' experiences, and identifying bias in policies and procedures. You may also be required to develop DEI policies that foster equitable and inclusive practices implemented through your framework. Policies are the most effective way to implement sustainable DEI practices. Policies such as anti-harassment and religious accommodations can be implemented to protect employee rights and to promote inclusiveness. According to figure (Add), creating an anti-harassment policy includes thoroughly explaining conduct, proper investigations, and follow-up.

Figure 9.1   Creating an anti-harrassment policy

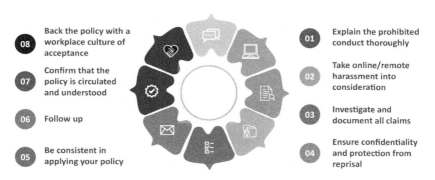

Source: Boatman, Andrea. "How to Create an Anti-Harassment Policy: A Practical Guide." AIHR (blog), February 16, 2022. https://www.aihr.com/blog/anti-harassment-policy/.

Leaders can also advocate for DEI policies in local, state, and federal government by promoting DEI laws. For example, in New York State, the governor implemented Executive order 187 to combat harassment and discrimination in the workplace by ensuring the proper investigation of complaints related to protected classes in government agencies.

After you've been able to appropriately gauge the needs of the organization, creating an effective strategy is next. The strategic plan or framework, as mentioned above, should outline the initiatives and actions you plan to take to advance DEI on your team like new policies and educational plans. Even if you don't lead the DEI function within your organization, as an inclusive leader, you should have a clear plan for your team and/or area of influence within the organization.

Once you've begun to implement your framework, you want to ensure there is an evaluation process in place to assess progress and impact. As already mentioned, regular review is important, along with feedback from team members to help ensure accountability. One of your top goals for this plan should be sustainability. The strategic framework should be one that exceeds your tenure and can easily be implemented by others.

9.1.2 A DEI framework to support inclusive leadership

One of your main roles as an inclusive leader is to provide context for the DEI framework you want to implement. This context can be explained in several ways. It's important that stakeholders understand the framework isn't just a document that acknowledges diversity; but, it requires intentional steps to cultivate an environment where everyone has access to opportunity. When the framework is properly developed, it will help move the organization toward dismantling systemic barriers that perpetuate the oppression of certain groups. The framework will also cover overall outcomes.[84]

As an inclusive leader, an effective framework will provide you with the tools needed to strategically address the conscious and unconscious biases that impede inclusion and equity in workplaces. There should be ongoing learning and development that helps team members understand and identify the many dimensions of diversity and how they intercept and impact the way people work, communicate, and engage in the workplace.

An increase in awareness will promote empathy and understanding towards responses to people's issues within the organization. As an inclusive leader equipped with the proper DEI knowledge and tools, you will be better able to advocate for policies and practices that support a truly inclusive workforce, including equitable hiring practices, inclusive benefits, and access to opportunities.

9.2 Gaining Buy-in from Senior Leadership

In my experience as a DEI leader, I have found that gaining the approval and investment from senior leadership to be the most difficult task for inclusive leaders. However, this is the most important step in the framework.

First, you must be able to clearly communicate the business case for inclusion on your team and within your organization. This will start with sharing recent research and case studies that demonstrate how companies implementing these practices have increased innovation, employee engagement, and finances.

---

[84]. Lingras, Katherine A., M. Elizabeth Alexander, and Danielle M. Vrieze. "Diversity, equity, and inclusion efforts at a departmental level: building a committee as a vehicle for advancing progress." *Journal of Clinical Psychology in Medical Settings* (2021): 1-24.

It's important that senior leaders understand the importance of the work as well as the potential benefits to the organization. You want to also ensure that your proposal aligns with the core values of the organization and how inclusion will elevate those values and positively impact the overall business strategy.[85] Following are some ways in which you can get the support of the senior leadership in your initiatives.

9.2.1 Engage leaders at the start

Once you've gained full support and investment from senior leadership, it's important to engage the next level of leaders, as they will be the true catalysts for change around DEI within your organization. These may be your peers or next-level leaders. It's important to ensure these leaders understand the DEI vision and how it can work within their area of the business. You can share your vision with them in several different ways such as through training, focus groups, and team meetings.

It would also be best to include them in the development of the framework. Their voices and input will give them a participatory role in the process and contribute to developing a sense of ownership and commitment. This will also be an opportunity to identify collaborators and champions who can help you develop a network of like-minded individuals.

9.2.2 Ensure the plan is sustainable

A key feature of your framework should be its ability to sustain over time and tenures. This will be achievable depending on how robusticity of your plan. The plan should

---

[85]. King, Eden B. *Diversity, Equity, and Inclusion Insights in Practice*. 1st ed. Research in Social Issues in Management Series. Charlotte, NC: Information Age Publishing, Incorporated, 2024.

entail implementation steps, accountability protocols, and success measures. Also, your framework should have guidance for evaluation, tracking, and reporting. Another key component of your plan should include continuous learning structures. A strong network of like-minded leaders will also be important to continuing the work over time. When leaders are role models of inclusion, they will inspire trust and engagement in their teams and cultivate a more inclusive and equitable workplace.

9.3 Vetting and Communicating Your DEI Framework

The best way to vet your DEI framework is to create a communication plan. Creating a communication plan involves several key steps to ensure that the strategies are thoroughly evaluated, clearly communicated, and effectively implemented. Below are some steps you can take to ensure your plan is appropriately vetted:

Step 1: Establish clear objectives

Your communication plan should be designed to help others understand the overall goals of your framework. You may want to share information like how your plan will improve organizational culture, collaboration, retention, and engagement. You may also want to state how your plan will benefit the organization's main goals and performance. Clearly stating the goals of the plan will be the cornerstone of this process and measure its overall effectiveness.

Step 2: Determine stakeholders

Next, clearly identifying stakeholders based on how they may impact or be impacted by the framework is imperative. This will more than likely include all of the employees in the organization with a special focus on leadership, HR, and other people managers. Understanding the perspective of each stakeholder will allow you to properly tailor your messages.

Step 3: Develop key messages

Now it's time to create the messaging that presents your framework to stakeholders. These messages should clearly define the purpose, goals, rewards, and expectations of increasing a sense of inclusion within the organization. It's important that this communication connects the relationship between the framework and organizational goals. It should also include safeguards for a lack of understanding and acceptance.

Step 4: Choose communication channels

Select appropriate communication channels to reach different stakeholders effectively. Options may include email updates, team meetings, company newsletters, intranet postings, and workshops. Consider the preferences and habits of your audience when choosing channels to ensure maximum engagement.

Step 5: Create a timeline

Once you have a clear idea of the messages you want to deliver, it's important to create a timeline to ensure that information is set across the organization within an appropriate time frame. You should provide information such as announcing the framework, providing awareness about what it is, and collecting feedback from stakeholders.

Step 6: Pilot the framework

Before sharing your plan with all of your stakeholders, you should pilot it. This can include rolling the framework out in phases to get feedback from stakeholders at different times. This will help identify gaps or areas for improvement and course correction before sharing with all stakeholders.

Step 7: Provide training and resources

To gain and increase awareness of the framework you've created, it's important to offer training and informational material to all stakeholders based on their roles. This will be key in people understanding the strategy and their role in implementation.

Step 8: Collect feedback and iterate

Establishing a method for gathering feedback from stakeholders will be the next step in this process. This can be done through administering surveys or holding open forums to allow people to share insights on how the strategy is being received and changes that need to be made. Use this feedback to refine the communication plan and the inclusive leadership strategy itself.

Step 9: Monitor and evaluate

Continuously monitor the impact of the communication plan and your DEI framework. Evaluate progress against the initial objectives and adjust the plan as needed to ensure ongoing improvement and alignment with organizational values and goals.

Step 10: Rolling out your strategy

Now that you have vetted and created a communication plan for your framework, it is time to press the go button. This starts with implementing your framework across your organization and/or team. Using the multi-faceted approach discussed above, the leaders in your organization should have a strong commitment to the framework that includes an appropriate investment and accountability. As you roll out your strategy, it is important to be flexible and make necessary changes along the way.

9.4 Measuring Outcomes

Once you have fully implemented your DEI framework within your organization, you want to ensure that you are measuring the outcomes of your efforts. This should be done through a strategic approach to gather data that shows the Return on Investment (ROI) and areas where contingencies may need to be implemented. Start with identifying clear goals for your plan. For example: 100% of all employees will engage in a training that reviews the purpose of the framework. After six months of rolling out your strategy, you can measure this goal and determine whether it has been met or if other strategies need to be implemented to get you there.

Over time, other goals may include percentage increases in employee engagement, retention rates of diverse talent, improved team performance, and enhanced innovation. By setting specific, quantifiable targets, you can track your progress and share it with leadership.[86]

9.4.1 Developing metrics

Once the goals are established, it is crucial to develop robust metrics for measuring outcomes. These metrics should encompass both quantitative and qualitative data. Quantitative data can be derived from diversity demographics, turnover rates, participation rates in

---

[86]. Brancaccio-Taras, Loretta, Judy Awong-Taylor, Monica Linden, Kate Marley, C. Gary Reiness, and J. Akif Uzman. "The PULSE diversity equity and inclusion (DEI) rubric: a tool to help assess departmental DEI efforts." *Journal of microbiology & biology education* 23, no. 3 (2022): e00057-22.

engagement activities, promotion rates, and employee grievances. On the other hand, qualitative data will come from the lived experiences of the employees through their insights and perceptions of inclusion in the workplace. Using both datasets will allow you to gain a holistic picture of the effectiveness of the framework.[87]

9.4.2 Accessing ROI

In most cases, senior leaders want to understand how investments impact the financial performance of the organization. After implementation and tracking progress over a specified period of time, it's imperative that you be able to calculate the ROI of the framework. This can start with assessing the financial benefits gained from the activities, structures, and processes you implemented against the costs incurred. Some of the key areas you may want to focus on are increases in engagement, retention, hiring people of diverse backgrounds, and workplace satisfaction which contributes to financial performance.

To calculate the ROI of your efforts must quantify the results and compare them to the costs of implementing and maintaining the framework, such as ongoing training programs, diversity initiatives, and other investments. Completing an annual report will allow you to restrategize, build on the framework for relevancy and best practices, measure the success of your efforts, and track how they have improved the organization.

---

[87]. Johnson, Michael P., and George R. Chichirau. "Diversity, equity, and inclusion in operations research and analytics: A research agenda for scholarship, practice, and service." *Pushing the boundaries: Frontiers in impactful OR/OM research* (2020): 1-38.

Chapter Summary

- As an inclusive leader, it's important that you have the skills to build a DEI framework for your team and stakeholders.

- Once you've gained the green light from your leadership team, it's important to assess the strengths and weaknesses of the organization. Here, you will analyze (1) what the organization is doing around DEI and (2) how well they are doing it.

- When the framework is properly developed, it will help move the organization toward dismantling the systemic barriers that perpetuate the oppression of certain groups.

- You must be able to clearly communicate the business case for inclusion within your team and organization. This will start with sharing recent research and case studies that demonstrate how companies implementing these practices have increased innovation, employee engagement, and finances.

- The plan should entail implementation steps, accountability protocols, and success measures. Also, your framework should have guidance for evaluation, tracking, and reporting.

- Creating a communication plan involves several key steps to ensure that the strategies are thoroughly evaluated, clearly communicated, and effectively implemented.

- Once you have fully implemented your DEI framework within your organization, you want to ensure that you are measuring the outcomes of your efforts.

- After implementation and tracking progress over a specified period of time, it's imperative that you be able to calculate the ROI of the framework. This can start with assessing the financial benefits gained from the activities, structures, and processes you have implemented against the costs incurred.

Quiz

1. Why is having a framework important for an Inclusive Leader?

   a. To assist with creating an understanding of how DEI relates to the work you do and the people you lead and serve
   b. Promote an inclusive working environment where everyone can thrive
   c. Ensure the organizational commitment to DEI
   d. All the above

2. How do you make sure the organizational commitment to DEI is clear?

   a. Engage with the senior leaders within your organization to ensure alignment around how DEI will be defined and carried out within an organization
   b. This doesn't need to be confirmed
   c. The doesn't need to be a commitment
   d. All the above

3. As an inclusive leader, how can you ensure the commitment to DEI is not only spoken but also lived?

   a. Action is required
   b. That is the responsibility of senior leaders
   c. Holding self and others accountable
   d. All the above

4. What are the best ways to measure your organization's strengths and weaknesses around DEI?
   a. Workforce demographics
   b. Climate surveys to understand employees' experiences
   c. Review bias in policies and procedures
   d. All the above

5. What should be included in the strategic plan or framework?
   a. A framework isn't necessary
   b. The initiatives and actions you plan to take to advance DEI on your team
   c. It's HR's job to create the framework
   d. All the above

6. After accountability, what should be the main goal of your framework?
   a. Sustainability
   b. Compliance
   c. Respect
   d. All the above

7. The context of your framework is important because:
   a. Stakeholders need to understand the framework isn't just a document
   b. It will help to move the organization towards dismantling systemic barriers
   c. It ensures diverse experiences are not only welcomed but are also integrated into the decision-making processes
   d. All the above

8. When you properly develop an inclusion framework, you:
   a. Help move the organization toward dismantling systemic barriers
   b. Maintain the status quo
   c. Alienate certain groups of people
   d. All the above

9. What role should unconscious bias play in your framework?
   a. This does not need to be addressed
   b. This should be addressed by senior leaders
   c. It should provide you with the tools needed to strategically address the conscious and unconscious biases
   d. All the above

10. As new leaders join your team, how would you advise them to grow an inclusive mindset?
    a. They should engage in ongoing learning and development that helps team members understand and identify the many dimensions of diversity
    b. They should increase awareness to promote empathy and understanding
    c. They should be able to advocate for policies and practices that support a truly inclusive workforce
    d. All the above

Answers

1 – d	2 – a	3 – c	4 – d	5 – b
6 – a	7 – d	8 – a	9 – c	10 – d

Book Recap

The Role of DEI and Leadership

DEI and leadership

This book has been a deep dive into how leaders can grow an inclusive mindset and increase inclusivity in teams and within organizations. As discussed, building a culture that understands, respects, and embraces the principles that surround DEI is key. In order to do that, a leader must understand their role in strategically building a structure that educates, holds people accountable, and positively impacts the organization socially and financially.

Affirmative action

As an inclusive leader, it's important to understand the origins of race, racism, and social structures. Cultivating a general knowledge of the structures that have been used to systematically oppress and marginalize groups of people in the United States is imperative. Implemented in the 1960s, affirmative action is legislation that addresses discrimination in public settings like work and schools. It requires opportunities to be made available for people from underrepresented groups, like women, people of color, and people with diverse abilities. The policy has been a topic of debate for several decades. Today, we see anti-DEI laws having the same controversial impact on communities and workplaces.

Workplace Discrimination and Biases

As you implement your DEI framework, you'll notice that biases creep in. Throughout this book we learned that these biases can manifest in many different ways, below are some examples of the most common forms of biases in the workforce:

1. **Unconscious bias:** When someone unconsciously favors another who reminds them of their sister.
2. **Halo effect:** When someone is considered physically attractive, their intelligence or work ethic is also assumed to be high.
3. **Affinity bias:** When someone favors another person because it reminds them of themselves or someone else.
4. **Confirmation bias:** When someone looks for information that confirms their existing beliefs and ignores facts that challenge those beliefs.

Psychological safety

In this book, we discussed the importance of psychological safety, as it plays a vital role in fostering DEI in the workplace. As an inclusive leader, it is your responsibility to ensure that team members feel not only physically safe but also psychologically safe. When people feel safe in the space they are in, they will feel comfortable speaking up and sharing experiences. Open communication prevents unintended issues surrounding bias.

Leadership Identity

Determining your leadership identity is imperative to developing an inclusive mindset. As you evolve as an inclusive leader, you should continue to foster your leadership style, as it can lead to increased authenticity and purpose.

Cultural Intelligence

Being aware that other cultural norms exist and can greatly impact the way people communicate and build relationships is an important trait for an inclusive leader to have. This ability can be discussed as cultural intelligence or CQ throughout the book. As an inclusive leader, you must be able to adapt to different cultural norms and behave appropriately in diverse contexts. You must be willing to go beyond just acknowledging cultural differences; it also requires you to actively learn about different cultures and perspectives.

Power

The social construct of power is a key concept as you continue to develop your inclusive mindset. Power can have several different meanings. However, it can often refer to the ability or capacity to do something or act in a certain way. This can include physical strength, control over others, influence, authority, or even energy.

In relation to DEI, power can mean access to opportunities based on your physical or biological appearance. A clear concept of power will allow you to properly explain why the work of an inclusive leader is so important as it can be used in positive ways to bring about change and progress, or it can be used negatively to oppress or dominate others.

Leadership and Equity

Understanding equity is another important trait in an inclusive leader. Your goal as an inclusive leader should be to create work environments that reflect equity, fairness, and justice. However, being an inclusive leader is a growth process that will require you to use your voice to combat systemic biases and discrimination. Acquiring this important skill will help you build more effective teams and achieve organizational goals.

Communication and cultural inclusion

With the main goal being to empower all team members to be their best, communication among different cultures becomes a key strategy. This will allow team members to be open, build trust, and be more willing to collaborate. Inclusive leadership is not just about tolerating differences, but also actively embracing and celebrating those differences to improve the work environment and meet goals.

Fostering Purpose as a Leader

Purpose drives the motivation of an inclusive leader. Purpose is what will align the leader with the organization's vision and values as well as with those on their team. An inclusive leader with a clear purpose is more likely to embrace and create more inclusive spaces. Leaders with inclusion as a purpose not only welcome different perspectives but also intentionally seek them out and integrate them into the decision-making process.

Empathy

Leaders should also develop a habit of continuous learning and empathy. Acquiring the skills of empathy can be honed over time. There's no real beginning and ending point, but a commitment to continuous development. This continuous development can look like training, reading, and seeking feedback from others to enhance.

Developing effective teams

Inclusive leaders should be paying particular attention to fostering a culture of trust and mutual respect among all team members. This is best demonstrated through showing transparency in your decision-making processes and creating an inclusive environment. In practice, this looks like promoting teamwork and offering opportunities for professional development. As a leader, when you can put the success and welfare of your team at the forefront of all you do, you can build a cohesive and resilient team that flourishes and fosters respect.

ROI and frameworks

Moving the needle forward means using analytics to influence performance outcomes. When using data, you want to be able to explain how the numbers impact the organization, team, and individual.

A. **At the organizational level:** The focus should be on how your efforts positively influence the success of the organization. Examples of such are profitability, market share, customer satisfaction, and overall business growth. These measurements often occur over a long period of time. Organizational performance outcomes are typically measured over longer periods and reflect the collective efforts of all teams and individuals within the organization.

B. **Team performance:** Outcomes focus on assessing the effectiveness of a group of individuals working together towards a common goal. Key indicators at this level include team productivity, collaboration, communication, and the ability to meet deadlines and deliverables. Team performance outcomes are important for ensuring that groups are functioning cohesively and achieving their objectives efficiently.

C. **Individual performance:** Outcomes focus on each team member. This data will comprise things like individual productivity, quality of work, adherence to deadlines, skill development, and overall job satisfaction. Individual performance outcomes are essential for determining the performance of employees, providing feedback for improvement, and determining rewards and recognition.

Summary

- Building a culture that understands, respects, and embraces the principles that surround DEI is key.
- Cultivating a general knowledge of the structures that have been used to systematically oppress and marginalize groups of people in the United States is imperative.
- As an inclusive leader, it is your responsibility to ensure that team members feel not only physically safe but also psychologically safe.
- A clear concept of power will allow you to properly explain why the work of an inclusive leader is so important as it can be used in positive ways to bring about change

and progress, or it can be used negatively to oppress or dominate others.
- Your primary role as an inclusive leader is to promote equity, fairness, and justice within your organization.
- An inclusive leader with a clear purpose is more likely to embrace and create more inclusive spaces.

Glossary

Change Management Consultants: Professionals who assist organizations in transitioning smoothly during periods of change, focusing on strategies to improve adaptation and minimize resistance.

Chief Diversity Officers (CDOs): Senior executives responsible for overseeing diversity and inclusion initiatives within an organization, ensuring these principles are embedded in corporate culture and operations.

Climate Surveys: Studies of employees' perceptions and perspectives of an organization

Cross-cultural Communication: The practice of effectively exchanging information among people from diverse cultural backgrounds, which requires active listening and adaptive communication techniques.

Cultural Awareness: An understanding of how cultural differences impact interactions and decision-making in a diverse team setting, is crucial for effective leadership and communication.

Cultural Intelligence (CQ): The ability to understand and effectively navigate cultural differences in the workplace, enhancing leadership capacity to communicate and interact with diverse teams.

Diversity, Equity, and Inclusion (DEI): A set of collaborative strategies aimed at promoting diversity in the workplace, ensuring equitable practices, and creating inclusive settings where all individuals feel valued and empowered.

Equity-First Approaches in Leadership: Leadership strategies that prioritize fairness and equal access to opportunities and resources for all employees, eliminating bias and systemic barriers.

Inclusive Leadership: A leadership approach that values diverse perspectives, creating an environment of mutual respect and openness, fostering a sense of belonging and promoting open, effective communication within an organization.

Mentorship and Coaching: Programs designed to guide leaders and employees in their professional development, providing tailored advice and support to navigate workplace challenges.

Organizational Development Practitioners: Specialists who focus on improving the effectiveness and health of an organization by aligning strategy, processes, and people.

Participative Leadership: A collaborative leadership style where team members are involved in decision-making processes, increasing buy-in and commitment among stakeholders.

Psychological Safety: A work environment where employees feel comfortable expressing their ideas and concerns without fear of criticism or retaliation, fostering innovation and engagement.

Resilience and Adaptability: Skills that enable individuals to recover quickly from challenges and adapt to changing environments in a positive and effective manner.

Servant Leadership: A leadership style that prioritizes the well-being and development of team members, promoting an empowering and supportive work environment.

Strategic Human Resource Management: The proactive management of human resources aligned with an organization's strategic goals, focusing on longer-term workforce planning and development.

Talent Development Specialists: Experts who focus on identifying, nurturing, and maximizing the potential of employees through training and career advancement opportunities.

Transformational Leadership: A leadership style that focuses on inspiring and motivating employees to innovate and align personal values with organizational goals, enhancing engagement and performance.

Workplace Culture: The shared values, beliefs, and norms that influence the behavior and practices of employees within an organization. A positive workplace culture fosters collaboration, innovation, and job satisfaction.

Bibliography

1. Afridah, and Muhlisah Lubis. "The Role of Communication and Employee Engagement in Promoting Inclusion in the Workplace: A Case Study in the Creative Industry." *Feedback International Journal of Communication* 1, no. 1 (March 11, 2024): 1–15. https://doi.org/10.62569/fijc.v1i1.8.
2. Backmann, Julia, Rouven Kanitz, Amy Wei Tian, Patrick Hoffmann, and Martin Hoegl. "Cultural Gap Bridging in Multinational Teams." *Journal of International Business Studies* 51, no. 8 (October 1, 2020): 1283–1311. https://doi.org/10.1057/s41267-020-00310-4.
3. Benmira, Sihame, and Moyosolu Agboola. "Evolution of Leadership Theory." *BMJ Leader* 5, no. 1 (March 2021): 3–5. https://doi.org/10.1136/leader-2020-000296.
4. Bhat, Meghana Moorthy, Saghar Hosseini, Ahmed Hassan Awadallah, Paul Bennett, and Weisheng Li. "Say 'YES' to Positivity: Detecting Toxic Language in Workplace Communications." In *Findings of the Association for Computational Linguistics: EMNLP 2021*, edited by Marie-Francine Moens, Xuanjing Huang, Lucia Specia, and Scott Wen-tau Yih, 2017–29. Punta Cana, Dominican Republic: Association for Computational Linguistics, 2021. https://doi.org/10.18653/v1/2021.findings-emnlp.173.
5. Bødker, Keld, and Jesper Strandgaard Pedersen. "Workplace Cultures: Looking at Artifacts, Symbols and Practices." In *Design at Work*. CRC Press, 1991.
6. Bohonos, Jeremy W., and Stephanie Sisco. "Advocating for Social Justice, Equity, and Inclusion in the Workplace: An Agenda for Anti-racist Learning Organizations." *New Directions for Adult and Continuing Education* 2021, no. 170 (June 2021): 89–98. https://doi.org/10.1002/ace.20428.
7. Creary, Stephanie, Nancy Rothbard, and Jared Scruggs. "Improving Workplace Culture Through Evidence-Based Diversity, Equity and Inclusion Practice," 2021. https://doi.org/10.31234/osf.io/8zgt9.
8. Edmondson, Amy C., and Derrick P. Bransby. "Psychological Safety Comes of Age: Observed Themes in an Established Literature." *Annual Review of Organizational Psychology and Organizational Behavior* 10, no. 1 (January 23, 2023): 55–78. https://doi.org/10.1146/annurev-orgpsych-120920-055217.
9. Einola, Katja, and Mats Alvesson. "The Perils of Authentic Leadership Theory." *Leadership* 17, no. 4 (August 2021): 483–90. https://doi.org/10.1177/17427150211004059.
10. Eisenberger, Robert, Linda Rhoades Shanock, and Xueqi Wen. "Perceived Organizational Support: Why Caring About Employees Counts." *Annual Review of Organizational Psychology and Organizational Behavior* 7, no. 1 (January 21, 2020): 101–24. https://doi.org/10.1146/annurev-orgpsych-012119-044917.

11. Enterprises, © 2013-2024 SDS Global, and Inc All rights reserved. "SDS Global Enterprises, Inc. | A Strategic Development Solutions Firm." Accessed December 18, 2024. https://sds.drshirleydavis.com/.
12. "Evolution of Leadership Theory - ProQuest." Accessed December 18, 2024. https://www.proquest.com/openview/8ef90e9e0f00125742cbb72f0d13db2b/1?pq-origsite=gscholar&cbl=5161133.
13. Galli, Brian J. "The Relationship and Impact of Communication on Leadership: A Research Note." *International Journal of Applied Management Sciences and Engineering (IJAMSE)* 8, no. 1 (January 1, 2021): 1–11. https://doi.org/10.4018/IJAMSE.2021010101.
14. Ge, Yuanqin. "Psychological Safety, Employee Voice, and Work Engagement." *Social Behavior and Personality: An International Journal* 48, no. 3 (March 3, 2020): 1–7. https://doi.org/10.2224/sbp.8907.
15. Gist-Mackey, Angela N., and Abigail N. Kingsford. "Linguistic Inclusion: Challenging Implicit Classed Communication Bias in Interview Methods." *Management Communication Quarterly* 34, no. 3 (August 2020): 402–25. https://doi.org/10.1177/0893318920934128.
16. Hastings, Lindsay J., and Hannah M. Sunderman. "Assessing and Measuring Leadership Identity." *New Directions for Student Leadership* 2023, no. 178 (June 2023): 99–106. https://doi.org/10.1002/yd.20558.
17. Hebl, Mikki, Shannon K. Cheng, and Linnea C. Ng. "Modern Discrimination in Organizations." *Annual Review of Organizational Psychology and Organizational Behavior* 7, no. 1 (January 21, 2020): 257–82. https://doi.org/10.1146/annurev-orgpsych-012119-044948.
18. Holliday, Adrian. "Culture, Communication, Context, and Power." In *The Routledge Handbook of Language and Intercultural Communication*, 2nd ed. Routledge, 2020.
19. Huning, Tobias M., Kevin J. Hurt, and Rachel E. Frieder. "The Effect of Servant Leadership, Perceived Organizational Support, Job Satisfaction and Job Embeddedness on Turnover Intentions: An Empirical Investigation." *Evidence-Based HRM: A Global Forum for Empirical Scholarship* 8, no. 2 (January 1, 2020): 177–94. https://doi.org/10.1108/EBHRM-06-2019-0049.
20. Kim, Sehoon, Heesu Lee, and Timothy Paul Connerton. "How Psychological Safety Affects Team Performance: Mediating Role of Efficacy and Learning Behavior." *Frontiers in Psychology* 11 (July 24, 2020). https://doi.org/10.3389/fpsyg.2020.01581.
21. Kiradoo, Giriraj. "Diversity, Equity, and Inclusion in the Workplace: Strategies for Achieving and Sustaining a Diverse Workforce." SSRN Scholarly Paper. Rochester, NY, December 20, 2022. https://papers.ssrn.com/abstract=4392136.
22. Kuknor, Sunaina Chetan, and Shubhasheesh Bhattacharya. "Inclusive Leadership: New Age Leadership to Foster Organizational Inclusion." *European Journal of Training and Development* 46, no. 9 (January 1, 2020): 771–97. https://doi.org/10.1108/EJTD-07-2019-0132.

23. Kwon, Chang-kyu, Seung-hyun Han, and Aliki Nicolaides. "The Impact of Psychological Safety on Transformative Learning in the Workplace: A Quantitative Study." *Journal of Workplace Learning* 32, no. 7 (January 1, 2020): 533–47. https://doi.org/10.1108/JWL-04-2020-0057.

24. Lackner, Mario, Uwe Sunde, and Rudolf Winter-Ebmer. "COVID-19 and the Forces Behind Social Unrest." SSRN Scholarly Paper. Rochester, NY, November 1, 2021. https://papers.ssrn.com/abstract=4026599.

25. Lee, Yeunjae, and Jarim Kim. "Cultivating Employee Creativity through Strategic Internal Communication: The Role of Leadership, Symmetry, and Feedback Seeking Behaviors." *Public Relations Review* 47, no. 1 (March 1, 2021): 101998. https://doi.org/10.1016/j.pubrev.2020.101998.

26. Lippert-Rasmussen, Kasper. *Making Sense of Affirmative Action*. New York, NY: Oxford University press, 2020.

27. Liu, Chang-E., Shengxian Yu, Yahui Chen, and Wei He. "Supervision Incivility and Employee Psychological Safety in the Workplace." *International Journal of Environmental Research and Public Health* 17, no. 3 (January 2020): 840. https://doi.org/10.3390/ijerph17030840.

28. Madi Odeh, Rana B.S., Bader Yousef Obeidat, Mais Osama Jaradat, Ra'ed Masa'deh, and Muhammad Turki Alshurideh. "The Transformational Leadership Role in Achieving Organizational Resilience through Adaptive Cultures: The Case of Dubai Service Sector." *International Journal of Productivity and Performance Management* 72, no. 2 (January 1, 2021): 440–68. https://doi.org/10.1108/IJPPM-02-2021-0093.

29. Maheshwari, Anil K. "Workplace Well-Being From Development of Consciousness Through Purposeful Leadership." *Journal of Management, Spirituality & Religion* 21, no. 2 (March 1, 2024): 206–23. https://doi.org/10.51327/WFAX3436.

30. Marin, Andy. "Inclusion as New Property Right: The Equality Act and Modernizing Anti-Discrimination Laws." *University of the Pacific Law Review* 54 (2023): 507. https://heinonline.org/HOL/Page?handle=hein.journals/mcglr54&id=542&div=&collection=.

31. Masur, Kate. *Until Justice Be Done: America's First Civil Rights Movement, from the Revolution to Reconstruction*. First edition. New York: W. W. Norton & Company, 2021.

32. Metinyurt, Tuğba, Michelle C. Haynes-Baratz, and Meg A. Bond. "A Systematic Review of Interventions to Address Workplace Bias: What We Know, What We Don't, and Lessons Learned." *New Ideas in Psychology* 63 (December 1, 2021): 100879. https://doi.org/10.1016/j.newideapsych.2021.100879.

33. Moon, Kuk-Kyoung, and Robert K. Christensen. "Realizing the Performance Benefits of Workforce Diversity in the U.S. Federal Government: The Moderating Role of Diversity Climate." *Public Personnel Management* 49, no. 1 (March 2020): 141–65. https://doi.org/10.1177/0091026019848458.

34. Mor Barak, Michàlle E., Gil Luria, and Kim C. Brimhall. "What Leaders Say versus What They Do: Inclusive Leadership, Policy-Practice Decoupling, and the Anomaly of Climate for Inclusion." *Group & Organization Management* 47, no. 4 (August 2022): 840–71. https://doi.org/10.1177/10596011211005916.
35. Munir, Misbachul, and Samsul Arifin. "Organizational Culture and Impact on Improving Employee Performance." *Journal of Social Science Studies (JOS3)* 1, no. 2 (July 28, 2021): 65–68. https://doi.org/10.56348/jos3.v1i2.15.
36. Musheke, Mukelabai M., and Jackson Phiri. "The Effects of Effective Communication on Organizational Performance Based on the Systems Theory." *Open Journal of Business and Management* 9, no. 2 (February 22, 2021): 659–71. https://doi.org/10.4236/ojbm.2021.92034.
37. Nowack, Kenneth, and Paul Zak. "Empathy Enhancing Antidotes for Interpersonally Toxic Leaders." *Consulting Psychology Journal: Practice and Research* 72, no. 2 (2020): 119–33. https://doi.org/10.1037/cpb0000164.
38. O'Donovan, Róisín, and Eilish McAuliffe. "A Systematic Review Exploring the Content and Outcomes of Interventions to Improve Psychological Safety, Speaking up and Voice Behaviour." *BMC Health Services Research* 20, no. 1 (February 10, 2020): 101. https://doi.org/10.1186/s12913-020-4931-2.
39. Owen, Julie E. "Deepening Leadership Identity Development." *New Directions for Student Leadership*, 2023. https://doi.org/10.1002/yd.20550.
40. Pew Research Center. "Pew Research Center," December 17, 2024. https://www.pewresearch.org/.
41. Powers, N. Thompson. "Federal Procurement and Equal Employment Opportunity." *Law and Contemporary Problems* 29, no. 2 (1964): 468. https://doi.org/10.2307/1190808.
42. Rahman, Syahrir. "Emotional Intelligence and Leader Effectiveness : A Conceptual Paper." *International Journal of Innovation and Business Strategy (IJIBS)* 15, no. 2 (2021). https://ijibs.utm.my/index.php/ijibs/article/view/99.
43. Raslie, Humaira. "Gen Y and Gen Z Communication Style." *Studies of Applied Economics* 39, no. 1 (October 28, 2021). https://doi.org/10.25115/eea.v39i1.4268.
44. Review, Harvard Business, Robert W. Livingston, Laura Morgan Roberts, Joan C. Williams, and Anthony J. Mayo. *Racial Justice: The Insights You Need from Harvard Business Review*. Harvard Business Press, 2020.
45. Roberson, Quinetta, and Jamie L. Perry. "Inclusive Leadership in Thought and Action: A Thematic Analysis." *Group & Organization Management* 47, no. 4 (August 2022): 755–78. https://doi.org/10.1177/10596011211013161.
46. Saba, Tania, and Queen's University Irc. "Understanding Generational Differences in the Workplace: Findings and Conclusions," March 27, 2021. https://policycommons.net/artifacts/1934280/understanding-generational-differences-in-the-workplace/2686050/.
47. Saha, Surajit, Roshni Das, Weng Marc Lim, Satish Kumar, Ashish Malik, and Bharat Chillakuri. "Emotional Intelligence and Leadership: Insights for Leading

by Feeling in the Future of Work." *International Journal of Manpower* 44, no. 4 (January 1, 2023): 671–701. https://doi.org/10.1108/IJM-12-2021-0690.

48. Saputra, Farhan. "Leadership, Communication, and Work Motivation in Determining the Success of Professional Organizations." *Journal of Law, Politics and Humanities* 1, no. 2 (February 5, 2021): 59–70. https://doi.org/10.38035/jlph.v1i2.54.

49. Seo, G., J. Mathad, J. Downs, and L. Reif. "Closing the Gender Gap in Global Health Leadership and Why It Matters." *Annals of Global Health* 83, no. 1 (April 7, 2017): 203. https://doi.org/10.1016/j.aogh.2017.03.504.

50. Sherf, Elad N., Michael R. Parke, and Sofya Isaakyan. "Distinguishing Voice and Silence at Work: Unique Relationships with Perceived Impact, Psychological Safety, and Burnout." *Academy of Management Journal* 64, no. 1 (February 2021): 114–48. https://doi.org/10.5465/amj.2018.1428.

51. Siripipatthanakul, Supaprawat, Tamonwan Sitthipon, and Parichat Jaipong. "A Review of Cultural Intelligence for Today's Globalised World." SSRN Scholarly Paper. Rochester, NY, April 7, 2023. https://papers.ssrn.com/abstract=4412246.

52. Tamunomiebi, Miebaka Dagogo, and Ebere Chika John-Eke. "Workplace Diversity: Emerging Issues in Contemporary Reviews." *International Journal of Academic Research in Business and Social Sciences* 10, no. 2 (February 13, 2020): Pages 255-265. https://doi.org/10.6007/IJARBSS/v10-i2/6926.

53. Van Knippenberg, Daan. "Meaning-Based Leadership." *Organizational Psychology Review* 10, no. 1 (February 2020): 6–28. https://doi.org/10.1177/2041386619897618.

54. Van Knippenberg, Daan, and Wendy P. Van Ginkel. "A Diversity Mindset Perspective on Inclusive Leadership." *Group & Organization Management* 47, no. 4 (August 2022): 779–97. https://doi.org/10.1177/1059601121997229.

55. Veli Korkmaz, Ayfer, Marloes L. van Engen, Lena Knappert, and René Schalk. "About and beyond Leading Uniqueness and Belongingness: A Systematic Review of Inclusive Leadership Research." *Human Resource Management Review* 32, no. 4 (December 1, 2022): 100894. https://doi.org/10.1016/j.hrmr.2022.100894.

56. Wang, Kenneth T., and Michael Goh. "Cultural Intelligence." In *The Wiley Encyclopedia of Personality and Individual Differences*, edited by Bernardo J. Carducci, Christopher S. Nave, and Christopher S. Nave, 1st ed., 269–73. Wiley, 2020. https://doi.org/10.1002/9781118970843.ch310.

57. Wood, Reed, Gina Yannitell Reinhardt, Babak Rezaeedaryakenari, and Leah C. Windsor. "Resisting Lockdown: The Influence of COVID-19 Restrictions on Social Unrest." *International Studies Quarterly* 66, no. 2 (June 1, 2022). https://doi.org/10.1093/isq/sqac015.

58. Wuryani, E., A. Rodlib, S. Sutarsib, N. Dewib, and D. Arifb. "Analysis of Decision Support System on Situational Leadership Styles on Work Motivation and Employee Performance." *Management Science Letters* 11, no. 2 (2021): 365–72. https://m.growingscience.com/beta/

msl/4285-analysis-of-decision-support-system-on-situational-leadership-styles-on-work-motivation-and-employee-performance.html.

59. Yufeng, He, and Zhu Rui. "The Black Civil Rights Movement in America from 1950s to 1960s," 1058–65. Atlantis Press, 2021. https://doi.org/10.2991/assehr.k.211220.181.

60. Zeng, Hao, Lijing Zhao, and Yixuan Zhao. "Inclusive Leadership and Taking-Charge Behavior: Roles of Psychological Safety and Thriving at Work." *Frontiers in Psychology* 11 (February 20, 2020). https://doi.org/10.3389/fpsyg.2020.00062.

Further reading

Books

- "The Inclusion Dividend: Why Investing in Diversity & Inclusion Pays Off" by Mark Kaplan and Mason Donovan
- "The Fearless Organization: Creating Psychological Safety in the Workplace for Learning, Innovation, and Growth" by Amy C. Edmondson
- "Inclusive Leadership: The Definitive Guide to Developing and Executing an Impactful Diversity and Inclusion Strategy" by Charlotte Sweeney and Fleur Bothwick
- "Diversity and Inclusion in the Global Workplace: Aligning Initiatives with Strategic Business Goals" by Carlos Tasso Eira de Aquino and Robert W. Robertson
- "What Works: Gender Equality by Design" by Iris Bohnet
- "The Power of Inclusion: Unlock the Potential and Productivity of Your Workforce" by Michael C. Hyter and Judith L. Turnock
- "Blindspot: Hidden Biases of Good People" by Mahzarin Banaji and Anthony Greenwald
- "Dare to Lead: Brave Work. Tough Conversations. Whole Hearts." by Brené Brown
- "The Loudest Duck: Moving Beyond Diversity While Embracing Differences to Achieve Success at Work" by Laura A. Liswood
- "We Can't Talk about That at Work!: How to Talk about Race, Religion, Politics, and Other Polarizing Topics" by Mary-Frances Winters

Articles, Websites, and Webinars

- "Tips for Inclusive Leaders ." Tips for inclusive leadership | TED Talks
- Morriss, Frances Frei and Anne. "How to Be an Inclusive Leader." *Harvard Business Review*, November 16, 2020 https://hbr.org/webinar/2020/11/how-to-be-an-inclusive-leader.
- Forbes - The Importance of Cultural Intelligence in Leadership

NOTES

Made in United States
Orlando, FL
18 September 2025